The CHURCH encounters ASIA

The CHURCH encounters ASIA

by Spencer J. Palmer

Published By
Deseret Book Company
Salt Lake City, Utah
1970

LITHOGRAPHED BY

DESERET NEWS PRESS

IN THE UNITED STATES OF AMERICA

To
Gordon B. Hinckley

I want to testify to you that God was with us when we stood beneath that tree in old China when we dedicated that land to the preaching of the gospel. My words may not convince you of the fact, but no disputant can convince us that our souls were not filled to overflowing with the Spirit of God on that occasion.

David O. McKay
Report of a world tour, 1921

The signs of divinity are in the Far East. The work of the Almighty is increasing with a tremendous surge.

Harold B. Lee
General Conference Address, 1954

Are we going to preach the gospel in Korea, in Japan, in China, and to the other people of the Far East? Yes, we are. Why? Because the blood of Israel is there. And the Lord did just what he said he would do with Abraham and his posterity. He scattered them over the whole face of the earth.

Joseph Fielding Smith
At Brigham Young University, 1962

The Lord is pouring our his Spirit on the lands of Asia, and he is touching the hearts of many good people, ad whole nations will be blessed by reason of the outpouring of that Spirit. Within a generation we will have strength and power here, and the Lord's work will blossom and roll forth. And it will be wonderful to behold.

Gordon B. Hinckley
At the Seoul East Chapel, 1968

In the timetable of the Lord, I think that the door is now open and that this is the time for the work in Asia. Each visit there has been productive and inspirational. In each of the countries the tremendous expansion and growth is an inspiration.

Ezra Taft Benson
General Conference Address, 1970

Contents

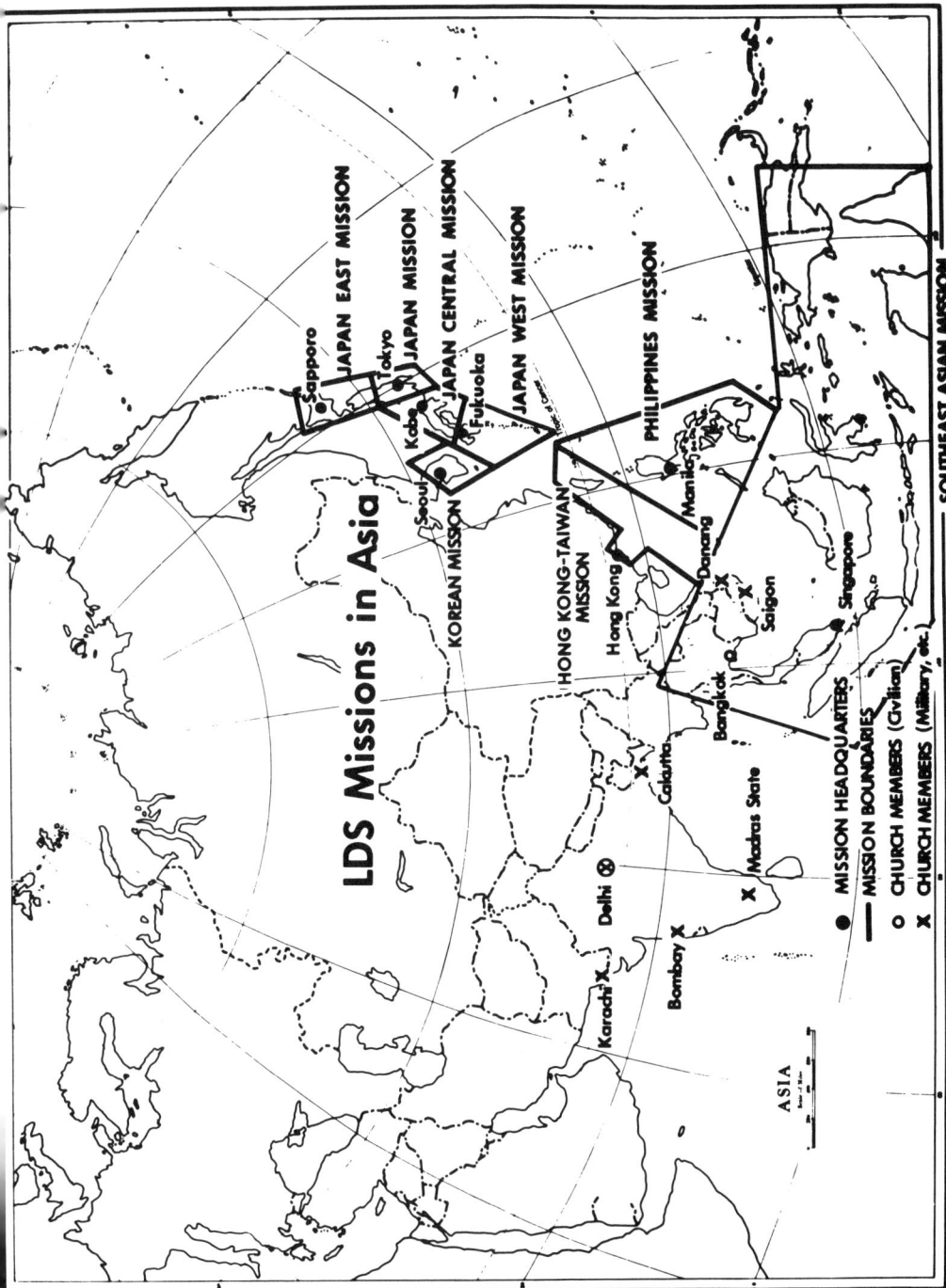

LDS Missions in Asia

JAPAN EAST MISSION
JAPAN MISSION
JAPAN CENTRAL MISSION
JAPAN WEST MISSION
PHILIPPINES MISSION
KOREAN MISSION
HONG KONG-TAIWAN MISSION
SOUTHEAST ASIAN MISSION

Sapporo
Tokyo
Kobe
Fukuoka
Seoul
Manila
Danang
Saigon
Singapore
Hong Kong
Bangkok
Calcutta
Madras State
Delhi
Bombay
Karachi

ASIA

● MISSION HEADQUARTERS
— MISSION BOUNDARIES
o CHURCH MEMBERS (Civilian)
X CHURCH MEMBERS (Military, etc.)

1

The CHURCH in ASIA today

The CHURCH
in ASIA today

The work of the Lord is moving forth in Asia. Truly, the Church is passing through an era of memorable and historic growth in that part of the world. Baptisms for 1969 exceeded by one hundred percent those of the previous year, and the trend has continued upward. In early 1970 two new missions were formed in Japan, bringing the total to four on the islands of Japan and Okinawa. A new Tokyo Stake of Zion, the first stake of the Church in the eastern hemisphere, was organized on Sunday, March 15.

A second Asian stake has been authorized for Manila, in the Philippines. No part of Asia has made greater progress in effective proselyting, development of leadership, and the promotion of the spirit of the gospel in the homes of the people than in the Philippines. It is estimated that of the fourteen hundred converts in 1969 and the estimated eight hundred for the first half of 1970, ninety percent will come into the Church as families.[1] Following a visit to Manila in March, 1970, Elder Ezra Taft Benson of the Council of the Twelve reported to the First Presidency:

> I spent all Saturday afternoon and evening in personal inter-
> views with leaders in the mission and district presidencies, district
> council, presidents of branches and elder's quorums. These are
> strong, humble men of ability—lawyers, engineers, government
> officials, educators, and retired military officers who are most
> teachable as fathers and priesthood bearers. Some have been to
> the temple, most all of them are saving and planning to go.

Other stakes to carry on the full program of the Church

---

[1]For the basic information contained in these introductory pages, the author wishes to acknowledge the kind assistance of Elder Ezra Taft Benson.

are expected to be organized by the General Authorities in other Asian countries. Seoul and Hong Kong are promising places in this regard. Anticipating the creation of a separate mission in Taiwan, the Brethren have already authorized construction of a new mission home for Taipei.

Japan now has over twelve thousand members of the Church. There are four thousand in Korea, nearly six thousand in the Philippines, some four thousand in Hong Kong, and more than that in Taiwan. Beginnings have been made in Thailand, Singapore, and Indonesia. There are strong Latter-day Saint congregations in Okinawa, and a nucleus of Vietnamese have come into the Church. Mormon servicemen in Korea laid the foundation for the Church there, and it is hoped that when peace comes to Vietnam, the gospel may be spread among that people. In Vietnam the servicemen are helping construct chapels and making friends and converts for the Church. There are three districts of Latter-day Saint servicemen in Vietnam, and some Vietnamese converts have already been ordained to the Melchizedek Priesthood. Latter-day Saint military personnel are also in Thailand, where more than a score full-time missionaries are laboring.

On October 29, 1969, the islands of Indonesia, with 130 million people, were dedicated for the preaching of the gospel, and the work has started with a few missionaries in Djakarta.

Singapore, dedicated for missionary work in May of 1969, has two branches with over three hundred average attendance. A new Southeast Asian mission has been established with headquarters in Singapore.

One of the great needs of the Church in Asia is buildings. On January 1, 1970, the entire Philippines Mission had only one chapel. Sites are being purchased and plans are going forward for additional buildings. A six-story building is reportedly planned by the First Presidency for central Tokyo. This could house a stake and ward facility, distribution center, mission offices, construction offices, and needed apartment facilities.

Indicative of the growth of the Church in Asia are the new Tokyo Stake, the two new Japanese missions, and the Church involvement in Expo '70.

Tokyo Stake

On Sunday, March 15, 1970, following interviews with mission and district leaders, Elders Ezra Taft Benson, Hugh B. Brown, and Gordon B. Hinckley of the Council of the Twelve organized the Tokyo Stake. Kenji Tanaka, project manager of the Nepon Company, an engineering firm in Tokyo, was sustained as president; Yashihiko Kikuchi, first counselor; and Kenichi Sagara, second counselor.

Also selected were a full high council, stake clerk, assistant stake clerk, executive secretary, stake mission presidency, a seventies group, and the presidencies of five elder's quorums.

Six wards within the radius of fifteen miles of Tokyo make up the new stake, with ward names and bishops as follows: Tokyo, Kazuo Imai; Tokyo 2nd, Yasuhiro Matsushita; Tokyo 3rd, Ryuichi Inoue; Tokyo 4th, Kiyoshi Sakai; Tokyo 5th, Noboru Kamio; and Yokohama, Genya Asama. These comprise a strong, compact stake, with a membership of four thousand under capable leadership.

For President Tanaka and the six bishops of his stake, a joyful sequel to the organization of the Tokyo Stake was their attendance at the 140th Annual General Conference of the Church in Salt Lake City, where they were privileged to receive instructions from the prophets of the Lord and had a special interview with the First Presidency of the Church.

President Tanaka reported that the happiness and warmth of this experience was equal only to the outpouring of God's Spirit eighteen years before in April of 1952, when he was first converted and baptized into the Church after years of painful and prayerful search.

New Japan Missions

Fighting recent heavy snow, rain and flooded roads, Elders Benson and Hinckley arrived on March 16, 1970, on the Island of Hokkaido at Sapporo, a city of a million population. They were there for a joyous meeting with the local saints and to create a new mission and introduce the new mission president. The matter of the division of the Japan Mission was

Russell Nozomi Horiuchi, first president of
the Japan East Mission, and his wife, Aiko.

presented and approved. President and Sister Russell N.
Horiuchi, formerly of the Brigham Young University faculty
and superbly qualified by experience to serve the Lord in
Japan, were introduced to preside over the new Japan East
Mission. According to Elder Benson's report: "This choice
couple won the hearts of the people immediately, as they had
done the day before at the Tokyo Conference."

Two days later the Japan West Mission was created from
a division of the Japan-Okinawa Mission. Prior to Elder Benson's arrival in Fukuoka, five experienced elders had arrived
and were helping launch the work of the new mission. A four-
bedroom Japanese home was rented for one year to house the
new mission president, Kan Watanabe, with his wife and five
children.

The meeting that evening was a time of rejoicing as the
division was proposed and the new mission president and his
family were presented. Elder Benson observed on that occasion:
"President Kan Watanabe has the love and confidence of the
saints, missionaries, and servicemen, many of whom he knows
well from serving as a counselor to three mission presidents
and traveling throughout Japan in that capacity and as director
of the Church's distribution and translation work. This humble
pair, who both have filled missions, have the spirit and ability
to provide strong leadership for this new mission."

Presidency of the Tokyo Stake: Yoshihiko Kikuchi, first counselor; Kenji Tanaka, president; Kenichi Sagara, second counselor.

Expo '70

The largest number of visitors ever to visit a Church pavilion was anticipated as plans were made for the Mormon Pavilion at the Expo '70 World's Fair in Japan. Five million people visited the Mormon Pavilion during the New York World's Fair. Realizing that the 1970 fair in Osaka would be the largest ever held in the world, the Church made plans for at least nine million. Elder Mark E. Petersen, chairman of the Church Information Committee, assisted by committee members Richard L. Evans and Gordon B. Hinckley, directed preparations.

The site of the Mormon Pavilion, one of the best locations at the fair, was selected by Elder Hinckley in association with President Adney Y. Komatsu of the Northern Far East Mission. The groundbreaking was an inspiration to those who attended. Elder Ezra Taft Benson was there, as well as the president of the fair, the director of the fair, a member of the Japanese cabinet responsible for the fair, the mayor of Osaka, and others. Each paid tribute to the Church and emphasized that man has always been searching for happiness, but that at Expo '70 the Mormons would tell the people how to find it through their theme, "Man's Search for Happiness." Publicity in the news media was excellent. The press conference the night before the groundbreaking attracted twenty-six representatives of press, radio, and television, and they kept Elder Benson busy answering questions for an hour and a half.

The pavilion subsequently constructed was a two-story structure with a fifty-foot tower, capped by an eight-foot, three-inch fiberglass replica of the Angel Moroni statue that crowns the Salt Lake Temple. Assigned to the pavilion were forty-eight missionaries from the Japan missions. Missionaries who spoke Chinese, Korean, Thai, and English would also serve as fair guides.

The Mormon Pavilion was officially dedicated on March 13, 1970, the day before the fair opened, in a ceremony conducted by Elders Benson, Brown, and Hinckley of the Council of the Twelve; Elder Bernard P. Brockbank, pavilion commissioner; Presidents Edward Y. Okazaki and Walter R. Bills of the Japan-Okinawa and Japan missions, and Elder Marvin S. Harding, the Far Eastern construction supervisor, who was the officially registered officer in charge and who carefully supervised the construction from the beginning.

Tours through the exhibit began on the lower floor, which was dominated by a copy of Thorvaldsen's classic statue of the Christus, the original of which is in Copenhagen, Denmark. The imposing marble replica was made in Italy and shipped to Japan. Visitors were also shown a photographic display entitled "The Church in Action." It had been fabricated in Tokyo so as to include scenes relating to the activities of Japanese Church members.

The basic story of the pavilion was that Christ is the Creator and Lord of this world and of all people. The upper floor included two theaters and four exhibit areas: (1) six paintings by Stan Galli of California depicting the creative periods, each $3\frac{1}{2}'$ x 5′ in size; (2) the purpose and plan of life, an adaptation of a panoramic painting used in previous Mormon exhibitions, but using Japanese people instead of Caucasians; (3) the life of Christ—his baptism, calling the fishermen, ordaining the twelve, the crucifixion, and the resurrection; and (4) the restoration of the gospel in the latter days. This last exhibition group included portrayals of the First Vision, of Moroni and Joseph

Smith, a replica of the Joseph Smith statue that is on Temple Square in Salt Lake City, and a painting by Dale Kilbourn of Salt Lake City of Heber J. Grant opening Japan for missionary work.

A printing of 500,000 specially illustrated copies of the Book of Mormon in Japanese was authorized for sale at the information area on the lower floor. Chinese and Korean editions were also available. Japanese editions of various tracts and pamphlets were prepared by the Translation Services Department of the Church in Tokyo, as were the following hardbound books: *The Articles of Faith* and *Jesus the Christ* (both also available in Chinese), *A Marvelous Work and a Wonder, What of the Mormons? Sing With Me,* and *Hymns of the Church.*

No doubt the high point of the entire exposition was the movie *Man's Search for Happiness,* which had been filmed on location in Japan, using native Japanese talent. Production of this movie especially for the Japanese represented a milestone in Church affairs and is a story of commanding interest. Its director, W. O. Whitaker, BYU Department of Motion Picture Production, gives the following account:

> The BYU Department of Motion Picture Production was commissioned by the General Authorities to produce *Man's Search for Happiness* with a Japanese cast in a Japanese setting. In the interest of economy, our first thought was to use a group of Nisei for the cast, and for locale, to select a possible site in San Francisco. No sooner had the word got around that this was to be the approach than we began to receive letters, telephone calls, and personal visits from Japanese people and others who understand the Orient, urging that the film be produced in Japan. It was pointed out that Nisei and Sansei (second- and third-generation American people of Japanese descent) have a noticeably different appearance from native-born Japanese, due principally to body build and bone structure. We were also cautioned that the native Japanese would never be fooled by a simulated locale. They would laugh or be disturbed at such an attempt, much as Americans are amused at the Japanese attempts to produce American-type westerns.
>
> The Brethren recognized these arguments as valid and gave approval for the film to be made in Japan. As a consequence, our crew, consisting of Robert Stum, cameraman, Douglas Johnson,

art director, and myself as director, flew directly to Japan to begin production in July, 1969.

One basic decision was to use the same music as was composed and recorded especially for the original film. It was felt that this music added much to the overall effectiveness of the production. We had heard that western music was very acceptable to the Japanese, a fact later substantiated while we were in Japan. It seemed that more western-type than Oriental music was broadcast on radio and television. However, use of the original music complicated our production problems, because we were locked into an exact timing situation, not only in the overall length but from scene to scene as well. The film had to hit emotional high points in exactly the right spots to match the music. I had to direct the production with a stop watch continually in my hand and to be constantly aware of the time element.

The script we took with us had been translated into the Japanese language in a rather prosaic, literal manner, and was much too long, due to basic construction differences in the languages. When some of the knowledgeable Japanese people read it, they could see that the language was somewhat wooden because of the too literal translation, and that a more poetic approach was needed. Fortunately, President Edward Y. Okazaki of the Japan-Okinawa Mission had introduced us to an unusual and talented woman, Kimiko Kojima, who was serving as councilwoman of the City of Ashia. Prior to her election, she had been a television actress and writer for a network in Osaka. Although not a member, she was friendly toward the Church and volunteered her help. She proved to be a great blessing to us; but for her, our project would have been much more difficult. She was able to revise and edit the script to the prescribed length under the watchful eye of Brother Kan Watanabe, in charge of the Church Translation Services in Japan, who checked it for doctrinal accuracy.

In addition to this great contribution, Mrs. Kojima introduced us to the heads of the Takarazuka Motion Picture Studio and assisted us in negotiating for the use of the studio facilities and personnel. Of course, we couldn't understand what she was saying to studio executives, but we were pleased to learn that she was bargaining with them to save us money. President Okazaki whispered in my ear that he was just going to let her talk—she was doing a much better job than he could do. She told them somewhat of the Mormon beliefs and missionary system; that President Oĸazaki, in being called to his assignment, had given up a lucrative position to head the mission without pay and received merely a living allowance; and that many of us serving with the BYU Department of Motion Picture Production had given up higher-paying jobs to work on such projects for the Church.

Apparently she impressed the Takarazuka people. The studio

Filming of the Japanese version of *Man's Search for Happiness:* Kimiko Kojima, member of Ashiya City Council, left; Keiko Amaji, female lead; Hisado Takeuchi, interpreter; W. O. Whitaker, director; Jiroshi Ogasawara, male lead.

head, Mr. Tanabe, indicated that he would do all he could to work us into their busy schedule and that because of the type of film we were producing, it was not his desire to make anything above expenses. We found him as good as his word, and our association with him and his fine staff in the ensuing weeks was an extremely pleasant and profitable experience.

During our negotiations studio personnel asked what kind of sets we would need. We answered that basically two sets were needed: one a hospital room and the other a Japanese home. At this they looked surprised and said, "Come with us." The meeting recessed for a few minutes while we visited Stage 2. Most of their sets were being dismantled except for two and, believe it or not, those two sets were just the ones we needed—a hospital room and a Japanese home! We were as astounded as they were. The fact that our sets did not have to be constructed lessened the strain on our budget considerably.

As work progressed on the film, our respect for our Japanese crew increased. We found them to be efficient and capable. While we could not communicate with them with words, we learned that there were other means of communication—principally the common denominators of experience and background. It was interesting to watch our art director, Douglas Johnson, make a few quick, simple sketches and see their art director comprehend immediately what we were striving for. Robert Stum, our cameraman, could make his explicit wants known completely to his Japanese cameraman by a simple motion of his hand; and the gaffers and grips (electricians and stagehands) would immediately catch the meaning of a nod and a gesture.

And so it was in my association with the actors. The key roles were carried by professionals, whom I found remarkably tractable and easy to work with. They didn't have to understand English to know what I was talking about. By walking through a scene once and doing a little pantomiming, I found it relatively easy to communicate my wishes. In the few places where our communications broke down, Takiushi-san, Mrs. Kojima's sister, would come to the rescue; she had a fair understanding of English and was helpful as an interpreter.

One of our concerns was to make this film in such a way as to retain the spirit of the original without making it offensive because of cultural differences. For instance, in the original we portrayed a Thanksgiving dinner situation. Now, what would we do to approximate this in Japan? We found that in Japan during the month of May they have what is known as "Boys' Day," in which the boys in the family are honored. We needed such an occasion so we could feature the formality of the traditional Japanese costumes, which are so colorful. Almost the only times the Japanese wear these costumes anymore are formal occasions such as Boys' Day. So Boys' Day permitted the mother to be in a kimono, the father and son in yukatas, and the grandpa in his native Japanese costume.

In the cemetery scene we had to be careful not to offend the Japanese but at the same time not compromise our Church doctrines. For instance, the Buddhists will bring to the cemetery, in addition to flowers, those things which the dead person especially liked in life, such as a particular kind of fruit. We staged the shot in such a manner that we were able to avoid the problem.

Our actors had been hired on a flat ten-day arrangement. We had figured that with good luck we could be finished in seven days. The extra three days were a contingency against bad weather. We had finished all of our interiors in seven days, with only one day of exterior shooting left to complete our assignment.

The day dawned on a beautiful, almost cloudless sky. Our crew set out for Kyoto, a two-hour drive, with high hopes of completing the project that day. As we approached our destination, the sky quickly clouded over and became overcast. We nervously waited for a hopeful sign that the weather would clear. Early in the afternoon we gave up and returned to home base.

The next morning we got an earlier start, hoping to outrun

any possible storm, but as we neared Kyoto, the clouds rolled tightly together as though a giant zipper had been pulled across the sky, and once again the day became miserable. It suddenly dawned on me—like a light turning on—that the Lord did not want us to use that location; and I also knew why. On one end of the island was a small, colorful Shinto shrine that would have been prominent in the picture. Nearby, standing on a spot the actors would have had to pass in the filming, was a stone Buddha several centuries old that sometime previously had been dredged up from the lake bottom. Neither of these would have been appropriate in the picture. We called off further shooting that day and decided to meet at an alternate location near the studio early the next morning.

We arose to a partially overcast sky. It was my turn to pray, and as we gathered the cast and crew together, I felt extremely humble and contrite. I reminded the Lord that if we didn't complete the production that day, we would be in grave difficulties, as our actors had other commitments that would keep them busy for several weeks. I had no sooner said amen than a rift appeared in the clouds and the sun came out. It wasn't long until the clouds disappeared entirely and we were able to complete our shooting.

I learned the great lesson that we should not try to impose our will on the Lord when he is trying to prompt us otherwise.

I had a number of preconceived ideas concerning Japan. One was that the people were extremely poor and willing to work all day for a few fish heads and a bowl of rice. Instead, I learned that they are prosperous with a high standard of living. We were all impressed by their industry and basic integrity.

One night as we sat in a small room of a restaurant eating a late dinner, a distinguished-looking Japanese gentleman with his wife and young son looked in. After we reassured him that it was not a private dinner party, he entered and sat near us. We remarked that he spoke excellent English and asked him where he had learned it so well. He told us that he was an importer from Tokyo and had many dealings with Americans, "although," he said with a smile, "my three years at Harvard University might have helped."

For an hour and a half we discussed with this gentleman such topics as economics, politics, and the unrest that seems to be common throughout the world. He then made the profound statement that what Japan in particular needed was more spirituality. He said that when Japan lost the war and Emperor Hirohito admitted that he was not a god, many people were disillusioned. Shintoism was the national religion, and the rug had been pulled out from under the people. Although they were basically a very spiritual-minded people, some of the Japanese had become agnostic and atheistic. He felt that the greater need in Japan was spiritual; they needed something to tie to.

Perhaps this is why our present missionary effort is so successful in Japan. We came away with the feeling that Japan has one of the greatest missionary potentials of any place in the world. The Japanese are basically a good people. When they fully accept the gospel, they go all the way.

Here is an example: For the film we had enlisted 30 people from a number of the branches in and around Kobe and Osaka to take part in the scenes of the premortal existence. Of course, white costumes had to be made. It was suggested that perhaps the one to take over this project was a member in Osaka who had a dress shop and was a fine seamstress. The time was limited—there were only ten days in which to complete 30 costumes—but she gladly accepted the responsibility and asked the help of a number of the Relief Society sisters from several branches in the area. One morning when we went in to talk to the sisters about the costumes, it was interesting to see this seamstress standing at the blackboard with about half a dozen women seated around her while she drew diagrams and sketches, very much like a football coach instructing the players in various plays. The costumes were finished on schedule. Of course we paid for the materials used and felt that since this was her profession, we should pay for her services also. When we asked for her bill, she said, "I am so grateful and feel so blessed to think that you would ask me to do this job, I would not think of taking any pay for it. I just feel that it is a blessing for me to be able to contribute my services."

The American elders and missionaries have little trouble making contacts, even on the streets. People will invariably stop when approached—in fact, they will even show up at the meetings they are invited to, if the elders can get a commitment from them. This is certainly different from the American's way of saying, "All right, I'll be there," and then going his way and thinking no more about it.

We had an interesting experience with the language. I was a little depressed after the first day of shooting because I didn't know whether I was communicating. We had a little free time after we were finished, and I wandered in to the stage next door to watch the filming of a TV production. The funny little Japanese director, who was wearing a turtle-necked sweater and a beret, would tuck his chin down into his chest and yell at the top of his voice, "Yo-ee!" and the crew and actors would snap to and get ready. Then he would say, "Kah-mer-ah [camera]." Next, instead of saying "Action" quietly as we do here, he'd yell out, "Start-o!" So I took my cue from him, and the next day I surprised the crew and actors with the same signals. They really jumped to, and from then on everything was peaches and cream. I was even saying "Kah-mer-ah" like the Japanese director. One day we needed batteries for some auxiliary lights on location, and when Bob Stum asked the studio helpers for them, they looked puzzled. Finally one of the men caught on:

"Oh, bah-tah-ree!" and from then on it was not "battery" it was "ba-tah-ree." We finally learned to communicate.

I would like to mention here the tremendous support we received from President and Sister Okazaki and their two fine sons. They spent many hours above and beyond the call of duty after regular mission hours to assist us where they could and help us get things we needed. We were touched to learn that the branches in and around Kobe, and perhaps some throughout the mission, held a special day of fasting and prayer for the success of the film.

During our stay in Osaka we visited the Expo '70 grounds, where many exhibits were under construction. We were greatly pleased to see the excellent location of the Mormon Pavilion. Certainly whoever made the decision was inspired, because it is near one of the main gates and right next door to Eastman Kodak's Pavilion. Of course, nobody at the world's fair ever misses the Kodak displays; they are among the better ones. Directly across from Kodak and the Mormon Pavilion is the huge Japanese Pavilion, which no Japanese will fail to see. So the Mormon Pavilion is situated right on the main concourse, with the likelihood that a tremendous number of people will go through because of its fine location.

It is our earnest and prayerful hope that the film will carry the influence it should for the Church. We were always conscious of this goal during the filming. And certainly if fasting and prayer and effort are of any avail, we should be satisfied with the results.

11

Christian Inroads

Christian Inroads

Christianity is not new in Asia. But the development of The Church of Jesus Christ of Latter-day Saints in that part of the world definitely is. Thus the Church naturally benefits from the experience and accomplishments of the historic Christian missions in Asia and is also unavoidably affected by whatever adverse influences they may have exerted there. Their work is of vital concern to us.

Catholic churches existed in the Philippine Islands even before European Christians first reached the United States. Some Protestant congregations in Indonesia are contemporary in their founding with the oldest churches in North America. In addition to these early beginnings, there has been a significant increase in the number of Christian communities in Asia, arising from long years of missionary work. The most recent figures available indicate that the number of Roman Catholics in Africa, Asia, Oceania, and the mission vicariates and prefectures in Latin America has grown to nearly 90,000,000.[1] The comparable figure for the total number of Protestants originally planted and fostered by western mission organizations shows an increase from 13,036,359 in 1937 to 27,160,000 in 1949, and to 60,114,082 in 1968. The Christian church membership increased 163% from 1911 to 1938, 53% from 1938 to 1949, and 266% from 1949 to 1968.

Great as these numbers may seem, they are misleading in a sense, because at any date a comparison of the Christian

---

[1]The statistical data presented here were kindly furnished by R. Pierce Beaver of the University of Chicago in a paper delivered at the Bergamo Mission Conference, Dayton, Ohio, entitled "Present Status of the Church in Traditional Mission Lands."

membership with the total population of Asia is a sobering experience, and the population explosion has destroyed any grounds for complacency. Taking Christianity as a whole—Roman, Orthodox, Eastern Catholics and Protestants—it now includes only 4.06% of the people of Asia. In predominately Islamic Western Asia the figure is only 2%, and that represents almost entirely Orthodox and Eastern churches dating from pre-Islamic times, not churches planted from the West. Even the Christian population of 13,178,200 in India represents only 3% of all the inhabitants of that land. The 6,607,000 Christians of Indonesia form just 6.8% of the population, although there are regions where they predominate, as in Minahassa, where Protestants claim considerably more than 90%. The Philippine Republic is the most conspicuous exception to the rule in Asia. Here is a country with a Christian history of 400 years and claiming a Christian majority of at least 85%. In Korea, where Christian growth has been miraculous, Christians make up a little less than 9% of the population. This compares with less than 1% among the Chinese and Japanese.[2]

It is generally conceded that if the population trends continue, Christians in the traditional Asian mission lands will steadily decrease in proportion to the overall population. Canon Douglas Webster[3] estimates that just to keep even, the newly established Christian churches must admit 15,000,000 members each year, and he does not see that happening. He states that one-third of the earth's people have not heard of Jesus Christ, one-third have heard something but have not responded, and one-third are Christian.

The Restored Church: A Worldwide Mission

The Church of Jesus Christ of Latter-day Saints is an expanding faith in a rapidly changing world. It has a divine commission to regenerate mankind and prepare the earth for the second coming of the Lord. The Prophet Joseph Smith

[2]Christian population figures for Northeast Asia are discussed in greater detail in Spencer J. Palmer, *Korea and Christianity: the Problem of Identification With Tradition* (Seoul: Hollym Publishers, 1967), v-viii. See especially pp. 109-10, note 8.
[3]Douglas Webster, *Local Church and World Mission* (New York: Seabur, 1964), p. 17.

emphasized the worldwide scope of the gospel message in these significant words:

> . . . the Standard of Truth has been erected; no unhallowed hand can stop the work from progressing; persecutions may rage, mobs may combine, armies may assemble, calumny may defame, but the truth of God will go forth boldly, nobly, and independent till it has penetrated every continent, visited every clime, swept every country, and sounded in every ear, till the purposes of God shall be accomplished, and the Great Jehovah shall say the work is done.[4]

The mandate is unequivocally clear. God's servants are commanded to proclaim restored truth to all men everywhere, for so the Lord has revealed in the preface to the Doctrine and Covenants:

> . . . the voice of the Lord is unto all men, and there is none to escape; and there is no eye that shall not see, neither ear that shall not hear, neither heart that shall not be penetrated.
> And the voice of warning shall be unto all people, by the mouths of my disciples, whom I have chosen in these last days.
> And they shall go forth and none shall stay them, for I the Lord have commanded them. (D&C 1:2, 4-5.)

The injunction is for authorized servants to be "sent forth to the east and the west, and to the north and the south," that

> every man might speak in the name of God the Lord, even the Savior of the world;
> That faith also might increase in the earth;
> That mine everlasting covenant might be established;
> That the fulness of my gospel might be proclaimed by the weak and simple unto the ends of the world. . . . (D&C 1:20-23.)

As Nephi once testified:

> Yea, and all the earth shall see the salvation of the Lord, saith the prophet; every nation, kindred, tongue and people shall be blessed. (1 Nephi 19:17.)

John the Revelator visualized the faithful in the last days glorifying their Savior in these words:

> Thou art worthy . . . for thou was slain, and hast redeemed us to God by thy blood out of every kindred, tongue, and people, and nation. (Revelation 5:9.)

---

[4]*Documentary History of the Church*, Vol. 4, p. 540.

Nephi also saw the conditions of the latter days, and recorded:

> . . . I beheld that the church of the Lamb, who were the saints of God, were also upon all the face of the earth. . . . (1 Nephi 14:12.)

Finally, in early pioneer times when the Church was almost entirely confined to the Rocky Mountains of the United States, President Brigham Young confidently proclaimed:

> Zion will extend eventually all over this earth of ours. There will be no nook or corner upon the earth but that will one day be in Zion, a part of the work of God. It will all be thus.[5]

Without doubt the Lord's commission to his church is to teach all nations. (Matthew 28:19.) Of course, this includes the world beyond Europe—the peoples and places of Asia.

Church Beginnings

At the time of the martyrdom of the Prophet Joseph Smith in 1844, The Church of Jesus Christ of Latter-day Saints had 40,000 members, and few expected it would ever have that many again. An early decline was again predicted with the passing of Brigham Young in 1877, even though the membership had by then reached 150,000. But owing primarily to the divine mission of the Church as carried out in a vigorous proselyting program, such gloomy forecasts are no longer heard today, as the Church enters the last quarter of the twentieth century with a worldwide membership approaching three million.

Before World War II this remarkable growth had been concentrated primarily in Utah, the western United States, and western Europe, in that order. But since that time, the most rapid expansion has been shifting from Europe to Latin America, South America, and the continent of Asia.

Church growth in Asia has been amazingly recent in time. In 1948 the Church had one mission there—in Japan.

---

[5]*Journal of Discourses,* Vol. 9, July 28, 1861, p. 138.

In the first annual report submitted that year by Edward L. Clissold, the mission president, membership consisted of a total of 153, listed as follows: elders, 7; priests, 19; teachers, 8; deacons, 16; members: male, 36, and females, 67. The Japan Mission was the only Asia mission at that time, and it is the only area in which the Church has had a relatively long history of involvement. President Clissold had arrived in Tokyo on March 6, 1948. By May of that year he had been able to renovate a partly burned house in Azabu, Tokyo, into a satisfactory mission home and to gain permission from the American occupation authorities for Mormon elders to enter Japan. The first group arrived in June and had to live with scattered Caucasian Saints. By late December 1948 there were seventeen American missionaries in Japan (including President and Sister Clissold), six of whom were first generation Americans of Japanese ancestry.

When President Clissold first arrived in March, a small group of Japanese Saints were meeting in a private home in Gotanda. About 50 children were also meeting at the home of a Brother Nara in Shimohitazawa. From these two groups and from later contacts made by the missionaries, Sunday Schools and cottage meetings were organized.

On October 22, 1948, Elders Harrison T. Price and Kojin Goya were assigned to Nagoya, where one Tatsui Sato was found to have been holding home Sunday School for over two years. Although the known membership of the Church did not exceed 200 by mid-1949, the *Church News* was able to report "an amazing reception" of the gospel in Japan, for more than 2,000 investigators were attending the several meetings.

Church growth in east Asia has proceeded at an impressive rate since that time. By 1957 there were approximately 1,500 members in several countries; in 1966 there were 21,000, and at the end of 1969 about 25,000.

The full story of the Church encounter in Asia cannot be covered within the pages of one book. Questions dealing with comparative religion—Mormonism and the native Oriental faiths—although of crucial import, must wait for elaboration elsewhere. But in the pages that follow, the missionary labors of countless Latter-day Saints who have prepared the way for today's promising harvest are set forth. They suggest, at least, that a vital, inspiring, and heroic beginning has already been made.

111

CHINA

CHINA

In August, 1852, only five years after the first band of pioneers arrived in Utah, President Brigham Young called the first Latter-day Saint missionaries to labor in Asia. At a special conference of the Church in the Salt Lake Tabernacle, nearly one hundred new missionaries were assigned to labor in many parts of the world: England, Ireland, Wales, France, Germany, Norway, Denmark, Gibralter, Africa (Cape of Good Hope), Nova Scotia, West Indies, British Guiana, large cities in the United States, Australia, the Sandwich Islands (Hawaii), and Asia. Of the missionaries assigned to Asia, nine were called to Calcutta, India ("Hindoostan"), and there probably were few more than that number in all the Church who knew for sure where Calcutta was. Four were sent to Siam (present-day Thailand), and four were called to labor in China.

Heber C. Kimball, of the First Presidency, gave a direct charge to those assembled:

> I say to those who are elected to go on Missions, go, if you never return; and commit what you have into the hands of God—your wives, your children, your brethren and your property.
>
> The missions we will call for during this Conference, are generally not to be very long ones; probably three to seven years will be as long as any man will be absent from his family.
>
> If any of the Elders refuse to go, they may expect that their wives will not live with them; for there is not a Mormon sister who would live with a man a day, who would refuse to go on a mission.[1]

Three of the four missionaries called to China reached Hong Kong April 27, 1853. The best known is Hosea Stout,

---

[1]Tabernacle address of August 28, 1852.

whose journals have been recently published by the University of Utah.[2] He and companions Chapman Duncan and James Lewis spent four months in Hong Kong. They tried unsuccessfully to move into the surrounding territory but found that the great Taip'ing revolution had cut off all avenues of successful missionary work. Stout reported that they looked to other ports in China, but that Hong Kong was the only safe place. A second, frequently lamented obstacle to their labor was the Chinese language. Because he was completely unable to speak to the natives, Stout maintained that he could not turn to the right nor to the left. "Furthermore," he said, "there was no resource perceivable for sustenance," and he concluded that they should return home as soon as opportunity permitted. After returning to San Francisco, Stout reported the seeming failure of their mission in a letter from which the following is extracted:

> We found about 250 Europeans or the Would-be-ba-bobs of the world, merchants, officers of the civil government (no common class which are found in English colonies and other parts of the world). This class we found almost unapproachable on account of their wealth and popularity and looked with contempt upon all who are not of the same grade with themselves; also a few lawyers, doctors, and a small sprinkling of missionaries also of the upper circles, luxuriating upon the cent society at home, and the miseries of the people in that region.
>
> There are about one thousand soldiers, the most of whom are Irish and Scotch, some English, some blacks from Ceylon . . . they are as corrupt as vicious habits can make them. The balance of the population is made up of four or five grades of Chinese, ranging from the merchants to the coolies who are carriers of burdens; also Malays, Lascars, Parsees, Portuguese, Negroes, Tartars, etc., a heterogeneous mass of tongues, manners, customs and religions.

A letter by Elder Lewis describes the people as caring little for anything pertaining to religion. He concluded his letter as follows:

> We then began to visit the people individually, so that we

---

[2]Juanita Brooks (ed.), *On the Mormon Frontier: The Diary of Hosea Stout,* 1964. The second volume of this two-volume work covers Stout's experiences relative to China missionary work. Additional details are available in *Autobiography of Hosea Stout,* edited by Reed A. Stout, 1962, reprinted from the *Utah Historical Quarterly.* 1962.

Hosea Stout, 1852, first Latter-day Saint missionary in China

might clear our garments and bear a faithful testimony, after having travelled so far. The heat of the atmosphere was very oppressive, being reduced in bad health owing to change of diet, the matter of preparing it and so forth, our spirits were becoming depressed and not perceiving a cheering ray of hope in all our labors. Our books were loaned and returned without thanks; our endeavors to teach the way of life and salvation were unheeded by the Americans and English. The soldiers turned away because of their officers and we seemed alone.

Andrew Jenson has observed that it is not known whether the elders made a single convert in China during their mission. But there is a report from Hong Kong that one young Chinese woman was baptized in the waters bordering that city.[3] At a conference held in Salt Lake April 8, 1853, Edward D. Wade and Cyrus Canfield were called on a mission to China. However, when they later learned that Stout and his companions had returned, they did not go.

In the Eleventh General Epistle of the First Presidency of the Church, issued on April 10, 1854, the China Mission is mentioned with the observation that the elders had left no impression on the empire.

In the winter of 1921 David O. McKay of the Council of the Twelve, in company with Hugh J. Cannon, traveled through eastern Asia on a special world tour for the Church. An important part of Brother McKay's mission was to visit China and, if he felt so impressed, to dedicate that vast realm for the preaching of the gospel. En route, these two brethren spent the Christmas season in Japan; in January they proceeded toward Peking, China, via Korea and Manchuria. The previously unpublished details of this historic experience are recounted by Elder Cannon in the descriptions that follow. It had been sixty-seven years since holders of the priesthood had been on assignment in China, and the first time they had been into the interior of that country. Thus Elder Cannon's account, which unfolds as if by a third party, provides wonderful insights into the conditions of that day:

A Quick Glance Through Korea

"The transition from bright and colorful Japan, an

3*Millennial Star,* Vol. 17, June 26, 1855, p. 607.

aggressive and virile world power in the making, to somber and gloomy China, a nation of decay and senility, is less abrupt because the traveler passes enroute through Korea, an intermediate country less cheerful than the one and less funereal than the other.

"Landing in Fusan [present-day Pusan], Korea, the visitors felt they were in another world, and their hasty journey through that land to Mukden, Manchuria, accentuated the feeling. The bearing and dress of the people, especially their strange and varied headgear, the clusters of homes whose color and shape make a village in the distance look like a group of toadstools, all awaken a desire to tarry and become better acquainted. Nor are the sterile, rocky stretches of land and the bleak mountains without interest, though not approaching Japan in point of beauty. Roads appear to consist mainly of foot paths and the transportation of the country seems to be carried on the backs of cows and oxen. Yonder an immense load of straw moved along the path without any visible means of locomotion, but somewhere under the mass was a patient cow. At the same time the driver, trudging along on foot, had a huge load on his own back.

"Straw appears to be the country's chief building material, as from it practically all the roofs and many of the sides of the houses in the country districts are constructed."

Into Manchuria

"At Mukden it was necessary to change money into Chinese, a task approached with considerable trepidation, as travelers are warned against counterfeit money with which China is flooded. Not only was the bogus article a serious menace to the uninitiated, but bills issued by supposedly reputable banks had little or no value outside of the bank's particular district.

"Brother McKay undertook to attend to this business while his companion secured railroad accommodations. The latter task was completed first and Brother Cannon found his chief standing somewhat uncertainly before the stoical Chinese money changer who had a 'take it or leave it' look on his

David O. McKay in Chōsen, [Korea,] in 1921

face. Brother McKay justly felt that the man was robbing him, and his Scotch blood rises in instant and vigorous rebellion at such thought. At this moment an American, who was leaving China and who had been making desperate efforts to exchange Chinese money for good American dollars, came up. The money changer's face lost some of its placidity as he saw his profits vanish while the fellow-countrymen carried on their own negotiations. Not only was considerable money saved in the exchange but this gentleman gave information which subsequently was of great value to the travelers.

"A glance at his map will show the reader that Mukden is far to the north and naturally in midwinter is extremely cold. From here the brethren entered China proper, another new world. And a ragged, dirty, starving, benighted and altogether forbidding world it was. On that part of the country through which they traveled practically no rain had fallen for two years and at the stations they were besieged by beggars whose pinched features and half-clothed bodies bore pitiful evidence of intense suffering.

"A stop was made at Shanhaikuan, where so much fighting had been done during the present revolution. Here the missionaries caught their first glimpse of the great wall of China, one of the marvels of all time. A British engineer has figured that it contains enough material to build a wall six feet high and two feet thick which would reach around the world at the equator. As the train was to remain there for a short time the missionaries started out to obtain a nearer view of the wall and perhaps a picture, when they were so beset by hordes of beggars that further progress was impossible. Though the weather was but little if any above zero, these pitiable creatures were nearly naked. It would be a compliment to call them ragged, and if some of them were not really starving they were past masters in the art of deceiving.

Peking and the Dedication of China

"Enroute from Mukden to Peking many Japanese soldiers were seen along the railway line and in their hearts the travelers rather resented what seemed to be an unwarranted intrusion. But at one station, and much to their surprise, they saw an American flag and a group of real U.S. soldier boys. Their surprise hardly equaled that of one young chap as Brother McKay gave him a bear hug, which, however, pleased him greatly after his astonishment had subsided. Though China at that time was comparatively peaceful, foreign powers were guarding the railway lines. This reconciled the visitors somewhat to the sight of the Japanese soldiers.

"Think of a city of a million inhabitants without a street car or omnibus line! The principal means of transportation—indeed the only means except for one's legs and an occasional auto or a small horse-drawn carriage at the time of this visit—were the innumerable rikishas. These flit rapidly and silently through crowded streets, dexterously avoiding collisions which to the traveler appear wholly unavoidable and furnish an excellent opportunity of seeing Chinese life. A facetious American has dubbed these conveyances pull-man cars. This was Peking.

"These brethren can never think of January 9, 1921, without a feeling of deep solemnity. As they approached the city on the previous evening they had looked in vain for a suitable spot away from the turmoil of the place where the dedicatory prayer could be offered should Brother McKay feel so impressed. Nothing but barren fields was to be seen. As the following day was Sunday it was deemed the fitting time to attend to this duty, if it were to be done at all, and Peking seemed the proper place. The hordes of insistent and repulsive beggars made anything but a favorable impression. One could hardly restrain the thought that preaching the Gospel to them was in reality 'casting pearls before swine.'

"However, with morning came a strong impression that the land should be dedicated for this purpose. But where to find a suitable place for the fulfillment of this duty was a serious question. It was felt that such a prayer should be offered under the blue heavens and in quiet, and from what they had seen of the city no such spot existed. Naturally this duty might have been performed in a room of the hotel, but who could tell what gross sins might have been committed there?

David O. McKay at Peking for the dedication of China

"It was an intensely cold though bright and clear winter morning as the missionaries went out into the narrow, crooked streets crowded with chattering and for the most part squalid Chinese. Placing themselves in the hands of the Lord to lead them as He saw fit, they walked almost directly to the walls of the 'Forbidden City,' the former home of emperors and nobility. Entering the gate they walked past shrines, pagodas and temples fast falling to decay, as all else in China is, and came to a grove of what they took to be cypress trees. A hallowed and reverential feeling was upon them. It was one of those occasions which at rare intervals come to mortals when they are surrounded by a Presence so sacred that human words would be disturbing. The brethren were very sure unseen holy beings were directing their footsteps.

"On the way to this grove many people were passed, but the number gradually diminished as they reached its borders. In it only two men were to be seen, and these left almost immediately. There, in the heart of the capital of the most populous nation in the world, unnoticed and undisturbed by the multitudes who were almost within a stone's throw of them, they supplicated the Lord for his blessing, after which Brother McKay offered the dedicatory prayer which in substance was as follows:

> Our Heavenly Father: In deep humility and gratitude, we thy servants approach thee in prayer and supplication on this most solemn and momentous occasion. We pray thee to draw near unto us, to grant us the peace asked for in the opening prayer by Brother Cannon; and to let the channel of communication between thee and us be open, that thy word may be spoken, and thy will be done. We pray for forgiveness of any folly, weakness or lightmindedness that it may not stand between us and the rich outpouring of thy Holy Spirit. Holy Father, grant us thy peace and thy inspiration, and may we not be disturbed during this solemn service.
>
> For thy kind protection and watchful care over us in our travels by land and by sea, we render our sincere gratitude. We are grateful, too, for the fellowship and brotherly love we have one for the other, that our hearts beat as one, and that we stand before thee this holy Sabbath day with clean hands, pure hearts, and with our minds free from all worldly cares.
>
> Though keenly aware of the great responsibility this special mission entails, yet we are thankful that thou hast called

us to perform it. Heavenly Father, make us equal, we beseech thee, to every duty and task. As we visit thy Missions in the various parts of the world, give us keen insight into the conditions and needs of each, and bestow upon us in rich abundance the gift of discernment.

With grateful hearts, we acknowledge thy guiding influence in our travels to this great land of China, and particularly to this quiet, and secluded spot in the heart of this ancient and crowded city. We pray that the petition setting this spot apart as a place of prayer and dedication may be granted by thee and that it may be held sacred in thy sight.

Holy Father, we rejoice in the knowledge of the Truth, and in the restoration of the Gospel of the Redeemer. We praise thy name for having revealed thyself and thine Only Begotten Son to thy servant, Joseph the Prophet, and that through thy revelations the Church, in its purity and perfection, was established in these last days, for the happiness and eternal salvation of the human family. We thank thee for the Priesthood, which gives men authority to officiate in thy holy name.

In this land there are millions who know not thee nor thy work, who are bound by the fetters of superstition and false doctrine, and who have never been given the opportunity even of hearing the true message of their Redeemer. Countless millions have died in ignorance of thy plan of life and salvation. We feel deeply impressed with the realization that the time has come when the light of the glorious gospel should begin to shine through the dense darkness that has enshrouded this nation for ages.

To this end, therefore, by the authority of the Holy Apostleship, I dedicate and consecrate and set apart the Chinese Realm for the preaching of the Gospel of Jesus Christ as restored in this dispensation through the Prophet Joseph Smith. By this act, shall the key be turned that unlocks the door through which thy chosen servants shall enter with Glad Tidings of Great Joy to this benighted and senile nation. That their message may be given in peace, we beseech thee, O God, to stabilize the Chinese government. Thou knowest how it is torn with dissension at the present time, and how faction contends against faction to the oppression of the people and the strangling of the nation's life. Holy Father, may peace and stability be established throughout this republic, if not by the present government, then through the intervention of the allied powers of the civilized world.

Heavenly Father, manifest thy tender mercy toward thy suffering children throughout this famine-stricken realm! Stay the progress of pestilence, and may starvation and untimely death stalk no more through the land. Break the bands of superstition, and may the young men and young women come out of the darkness of the Past into the Glorious Light now shining among the children of men. Grant, our Father, that these young men and women may, through upright, virtuous lives, and prayerful study, be prepared and inclined to declare this message of salvation in their own tongue to their fellowmen. May their hearts, and the hearts of this people, be turned to their fathers that they may accept the opportunity offered them to bring salvation to the millions who have gone before.

May the Elders and Sisters whom thou shalt call to this land as missionaries have keen insight into the mental and spiritual state of the Chinese mind. Give them special power and ability to approach this people in such a manner as will make the proper appeal to them. We beseech thee, O God, to reveal to thy servants the best methods to adopt and the best plans to follow in establishing thy work among this ancient, tradition-steeped people. May the work prove joyous, and a rich harvest of honest souls bring that peace to the workers' hearts which surpasseth all understanding.

Remember thy servants, whom thou hast chosen to preside in Thy Church. We uphold and sustain before thee President Heber J. Grant who stands at the head at this time, and his counsellors, President Anthon H. Lund and President Charles W. Penrose. Bless them, we pray thee, with every needful blessing, and keep them one in all things pertaining to thy work. Likewise bless the Council of Twelve. May they continue to be one with the First Presidency. Remember the Presiding Bishopric, and all who preside in stakes, wards, quorums, organizations, temples, church schools, and missions. May the spirit of purity, peace, and energy characterize all thy organizations.

Heavenly Father, be kind to our Loved Ones from whom we are now separated. Let thy Holy Spirit abide in our homes, that sickness, disease and death may not enter therein.

Hear us, O Kind and Heavenly Father, we implore thee, and open the door for the preaching of thy Gospel from one end of this realm to the other, and may thy servants who declare this message be especially blest and directed by thee. May thy kingdom come, and thy will be done speedily here on earth among all peoples, kindreds and tongues preparatory to the winding up scenes of these latter days!

And while we behold thy guiding hand through it all, we shall ascribe unto thee the praise, the glory and the honor, through Jesus Christ our Lord and Redeemer,

Amen.

"The brethren felt that this prayer was acceptable to the Almighty. His spirit gave approving testimony and at the same time revealed for their comfort and blessing some things which should transpire in the future.

"Poor old China, the victim of intrigues among nations who covet her coal and iron deposits, the victim of floods and droughts, of famines and pestilence, and worst of all, the victim of her own inefficiency and helplessness! Assuredly she needs someone to plead her cause before the throne of grace. China is living in the dead past of two thousand years and has hardly begun to realize it.

"And still her condition is not hopeless. She is as one passing through travail. A new nation, let us hope, is being born, a nation of great potential power, with leaders sufficiently wise to develop and properly exploit her natural resources. Among this people are hosts of splendid individuals, men and women of stable character, of refinement and intelligence. That many of them will accept the truth when it is presented to them cannot be doubted, if one may judge from the faithful Latter-day Saints of that race who have joined the Church in Hawaii and Samoa."

The First Chinese Mission

Elder Matthew Cowley of the Council of the Twelve, with a few others, stood on the "Peak," the highest elevation in Hong Kong, on July 14, 1949, to invoke the blessings of the Lord upon their labors as they started a preparatory work among the Chinese. With Elder and Sister Cowley were Hilton A. Robertson and Henry Wong Aki, a Chinese-American member of the Church from Honolulu, and their wives. Elder Robertson had been set apart as President of the China Mission, having previously presided over the Japan Mission until 1921, over the Central Pacific Mission with headquarters in Hawaii during 1936-40, and thereafter over missionary work among Chinese in Chinatown, San Francisco. He was to give longer service to the Oriental missions than any other man of this dispensation. Upon returning to the United States from this opening of the China Mission in July 1949, Elder Cowley reported:

I will never forget the prayer of Brother Henry Aki, who, as he stood there facing his homeland with its four hundred and sixty-five million inhabitants, poured out his soul to God that he might be the means of bringing salvation to his kindred people. What great odds, brothers and sisters, one man holding the Priesthood of God among four hundred and sixty-five million of his race! I was never so impressed with the preciousness of the Priesthood of God as I was when this dear Chinese brother, who felt the burden that was upon him, implored God to bring salvation to his people.

Between 1949 and 1951 mission headquarters were located at 345 Prince Edward Road, Hong Kong, and the work was begun. However, conditions were unsettled and the political climate was foreboding. President Robertson recorded in his diary in October, 1949:

This is the toughest assignment I have ever had; with no knowledge of the language, no members, neither friends, nor literature excepting the Bible and that, neither of us can read, not even Brother Aki. Then to help matters out a big war just over the back fence and the people anticipating a home run to be knocked over into our yard most any time.

En route to China aboard the *USS President Cleveland* for the reopening of missionary work among the Chinese (1949): front, Henry Wong Aki, Ivan Hall, Carolyn Robertson, and an LDS employee of the American President Lines; second row, Hilton A. Robertson, Sister Aki, Sister Robertson, Sister Cowley, and Elder Matthew Cowley of the Council of the Twelve; third row, an LDS employee of the American President Lines.

But the mission home served as a congenial haven for Church members in the Far East, particularly servicemen stationed there. The first two missionaries, H. Grant Heaton and William K. Paalani, arrived on February 25, 1950, and within a year eight elders were laboring in Hong Kong. Two baptismal services were held, and Chinese Church membership rose to seventeen. Study classes were conducted regularly, as were testimony and sacrament meetings on the Sabbath, with an average of thirty in attendance.

But progress was to stop. Proselyting in Hong Kong was interrupted by the outbreak of the Korean war in June, 1950, and the continuing revolution within China prevented further work. The missionaries were all withdrawn.

The Southern Far East Mission

In 1955, more than a century after the first missionaries called in 1852 by Brigham Young had arrived in Hong Kong, the Southern Far East Mission was organized from a division of the Northern Far East Mission. H. Grant Heaton was appointed as the first mission president. The new mission embraced the largest land area of any in the Church, reaching theoretically beyond Hong Kong and Taiwan into the Philippine Islands and all of Southeast Asia. Since this area included hundreds of millions of people of extremely varied linguistic, cultural, and racial backgrounds, the new mission president was forced to concentrate primarily on the Chinese who lived near at hand.

When missionary work among the Chinese people was reopened in 1955, not one word of Church literature had been printed in their language and was available to the public. Thus, as with all the newly established missions of the Church in East Asia since World War II, the most urgent problem was to resolve the language barrier. In late August, 1955, the first eight missionaries arrived to begin the task of language training. Six were assigned to learn the Cantonese dialect spoken in the Hong Kong area, and two were assigned to learn the northern Mandarin dialect spoken by Chinese in Taiwan. Eight more elders arrived during 1955. Ten hours language study per day were set aside. By the end of the year missionaries were sent out two by two to teach the native population. Their emphasis at first was with those Chinese in Hong Kong who could speak English.

It was felt that in addition to the missionary need for language training, the standard program of gospel lessons needed modification, or at least supplementing, in order to meet needs of investigators with non-Christian backgrounds. Thus, in November, 1955, a three-day conference was held to formulate a lesson plan adapted to the local situation. A systematic program of proselyting finally began, leading to the fulfillment of President McKay's prayer of dedication that the day would come when the Chinese people would break the "fetters of superstition and false doctrine" and that the "light of the glorious gospel should begin to shine through the dense darkness that has enshrouded this nation for ages."

During the four years of President Heaton's leadership of the Southern Far East Mission, there was an impressive increase in baptisms, especially after 1956, and unusual sensitivity toward the needs and problems of Chinese converts to the Church in such matters as cross cultural communication, social acceptance of the Mormon elders, economic conditions and living standards, health, and education.

A report prepared by President Heaton for Elder Mark E. Petersen of the Council of the Twelve, who visited the Asian missions in the early summer of 1959, reveals that by May of that year the mission had ninety-one full-time foreign elders and twelve full-time local missionaries; there were five organized proselyting districts with eight branches and an additional twelve groups. The first baptismal service for Chinese members in the new Southern Far East Mission was held on May 30, 1956, at the mission home in Hong Kong. Eleven persons were baptized, including three children. Five of the eleven were refugees from Communist China. Missionary activity between 1955-1959 was reported as follows:

	1955	1956	1957	1958	(up to May) 1959
Missionaries	16	40	57	83	103
Cottage Meetings	30	90	108	101	78
Baptisms	0	60	521	907	75
Church Owned Buildings	0	2	5	8	9

Membership activity in 1959 included 53% attendance at sacrament meeting; 52% attendance at Sunday School; 42% at MIA; and 45% at Relief Society. Average tithing and fast offering contributions were generally lower than the average attendance at meetings. Other vital membership statistics (including Guam service members) were as follows:

District	Male	Female	Deacon	Teacher
Hong Kong	180	114	12	7
Kowloon	348	146	23	2
New Territories	219	98	6	4
Taiwan	93	77	13	5
Guam	15	49	11	4
Totals	855	484	65	22

District	Priest	Elder	Children 8-12	Blessed but not Baptized
Hong Kong	4	3	22	16
Kowloon	9	5	21	5
New Territories	2	5	23	7
Taiwan	4	6	28	6
Guam	5	16	19	75
		(3)*		
Totals	24	38	113	109

Total membership 1,710

*Seventies

Elder Gordon B. Hinckley of the Council of the Twelve, who has spent more years as a supervisor of the Asian missions of the Church than any other General Authority, has said of President Grant Heaton:

> I first met H. Grant Heaton when he was called as one of the two missionaries to go to Hong Kong in 1950. Following the outbreak of the Korean war, President Robertson and his missionaries were transferred to San Francisco. Brother Heaton was subject to military service and because of his facility in learning Oriental languages was sent to Korea where his love for the Oriental people was strengthened, his heart being deeply touched by the suffering of the Korean children, many of whom were left orphans during the war.
>
> When the work was reopened in Hong Kong he and his wife were sent there. Their contribution can never be adequately measured. He spoke the languages of the people; he worked with them as one who loved them. He opened the work in the Philippines, and extended the work to Guam.
>
> Surely when any history is written concerning the teaching of the restored gospel in Asia, the name of Grant Heaton must be mentioned with appreciation.

Regarding President Heaton's successor, Robert Sherman Taylor, Elder Hinckley has remarked:

> Robert Sherman Taylor was called from his post as bishop of one of the wards of Hawaii to preside over the Southern Far East Mission. He faced a task most difficult. While he had learned to love the Oriental people of Hawaii, he did not speak their language. His predecessor, H. Grant Heaton, had spoken both Cantonese and Mandarin with facility. Nonetheless, President Taylor accepted the challenge and gave of himself unstintingly to the tremendous responsibility that was his.
>
> His devoted wife is a daughter of Edward L. Clissold, who had opened the work in Japan following the war, and she had grown up with a spirit of appreciation for the Oriental people.
>
> It was our experience to be in many meetings with them, including many testimony meetings, and to hear the missionaries speak of their great love of these people who had given so much in response to a call from the priesthood to build the kingdom of God in these ancient and delightful lands of Asia.

Under the leadership of President Taylor and Jay A. Quealy, Jr., who succeeded him, the mission expanded to include two districts in Hong Kong, three in Taiwan, and one in the Philippines, as well as servicemen's groups in the outlying areas of Vietnam, Burma, Laos, Malaysia, and Pakistan. The centers of missionary work, however, were still in Hong Kong and Taiwan.

Jay A. Quealy, Jr. First Church buildings in the Southern Far East Mission were constructed during his presidency.

Developments in Hong Kong

Hong Kong, a British Crown colony on the southeast coast of mainland China, has a population of about four million. Its residents are almost 98 percent Chinese, mostly of Cantonese and other groups found in neighboring Kuangtung Province of China, and include more than one million refugees. One of the most beautiful cities in the world, it is completely surrounded by water. From the standpoint of missionary work it is an interesting and challenging area.

There is much monetary need in Hong Kong—more so than in any of the other zones of the mission. The members themselves are in a highly competitive situation. They are people who, for the most part, have fled from their native land of mainland China, seeking freedom. Having left their material possessions behind, their greatest problem is the fight for survival. They are fighting for a place to live, fighting for food to eat, fighting for status in the Chinese social tradition. This makes it difficult for our Church members, because they are torn between their great drive for survival and their activity in the Church. Their ultimate success depends upon their adherence to the principles of the gospel.

When President Quealy arrived, Hong Kong was divided into three member districts, each of which was presided over by a missionary. Since local members were doing little in the running of the branches or the districts, one of the first tasks was to develop more local leadership.

The district was handled by the mission presidency, and there was no district president. Loh Ying Wah was called as counselor in the mission presidency, and a missionary was called as the other counselor. A district council was also created. At first it was made up of four local brethren and six missionaries. Gradually local leadership was increased until it was made up of eleven local brethren and one missionary— the assistant to the mission president.

At the beginning of 1965 it was decided that it was time to create a full-fledged member district. President Loh was sustained as the district president, with Ng Kat Hing as first counselor, Hui Tung Ching as second counselor, and Brother Malan Jackson, a former missionary who was employed at the Bank of America in Hong Kong, as the district clerk.

By mid-1965 all of the branches of the Hong Kong district were presided over by local Chinese brethren, with the exception of the Sha Tin and Sham Shui Po branches.

The Church owns all of its branch chapels in Hong Kong, most of them being located on the top floors of apartment house buildings. Kum Tong Hall, which was purchased by President Taylor just before his departure, is a particularly attractive building. Once the residence of a noted Chinese merchant, Sir Robert Tong, the structure is of reinforced concrete with red brick veneer, the brick having come from England. Its balconies afford a remarkable view of the harbor, and from them during World War II occupants watched the bombing and strafing by Japanese planes that led to the surrender of the colony and the trying years of Japanese occupation. This historic structure has been remodeled to include a chapel, cultural hall, classrooms, baptismal font, and elders' quarters.

The mission president's stately home, which serves as headquarters of the mission, is located at #2 Cornwall Road in Kowloon, on a choice piece of property.

It is of more than incidental interest that the mission presidents have encountered a good deal of trouble securing titles to the various properties the Church has purchased in the Hong Kong area.

Taiwan

Taiwan (Formosa), the seat of the Nationalist government since 1949, is an island ninety miles off the coast of the Chinese mainland, about three hundred miles northeast of Hong Kong. The capital is Taipei.

Taiwan has a population of more than 13.5 million; the neighboring Pescadores (Penghu) Islands a population of about 100,000; and the offshore islands a total of approximately 70,000 inhabitants, excluding the Nationalist military.

The Taiwanese, with the exception of about 150,000 aborigines believed to be related to the aboriginal tribes in the Philippines, are descendants of Chinese who migrated from the crowded coastal areas of Fukien and Kwangtung Provinces within the last three hundred years. The approximately 1.5 million mainlanders who arrived in Taiwan in 1949 and 1950 came from all parts of China.

Mormon missionary work in Taiwan started under the direction of President Heaton in 1959 and grew from a modest beginning to a membership in 1966 of approximately three thousand. The first missionaries to labor in Formosa were Duane W. Dean, Keith A. Madsen, Weldon J. Kitchen, and Melvin C. Rich, who studied Mandarin in Hong Kong nine months before going to Taiwan. Prior to their arrival, there was in Taipei an active servicemen's group, which was later

First Chinese chapel in Taiwan, at Taipei, was dedicated October 16, 1966, by Elder Gordon B. Hinckley of the Council of the Twelve.

organized into a branch.[4] Since missionary work has commenced, Taiwan has been divided into three districts—North Taiwan, South Taiwan, and the Central Taiwan districts.

A Chinese member from Taipei, Brother Hu Wei I, was called as counselor in the Southern Far East Mission presidency. His was the key role in translating the Book of Mormon into the Chinese language, and he is widely regarded for his devotion to the Church.

According to President Quealy, there were sixteen branches of the Church on Taiwan by 1965, eleven of which were presided over by local brethren and five by missionaries. At that time there were also a number of American servicemen, most of whom were in Taipei, with some in Kao Hsiung, T'ai Nan and T'ai Chung. They were a great benefit to the struggling new branches and to the eighty-three missionaries serving on the island at that time.

The first building constructed was the Taipei chapel, similar to a large stake center, which can seat approximately 1,600 to 1,800 persons in the combined chapel and cultural hall. Under the supervision of Karl Teeples, this building was completed for

[4]See *Church News,* June 23, 1956.

the use of two branches in Taipei. President Quealy has reported that financial donations and labor enabled the building to be completely paid for by the time it was finished. The devotion of these Saints is evident in the fact that the building was not occupied immediately after it was completed because they felt that it should be dedicated first.

The Church has been incorporated in Taiwan as an entity in the Republic of China with the First Presidency as the governing body and with the board of directors headed by the mission president. As in Korea, the mission in Taiwan has entered into an interesting arrangement with regard to several of the buildings it uses. The Church makes a deposit of a certain number of dollars with the landlord, then occupies the building with either a minimum rent or no rent at all, the interest from the deposit becoming the landlord's return. At the end of the prescribed period of time, the landlord returns the amount of deposit without any interest to the Church. The principal example of this arrangement in Taiwan is the old North Taipei Branch.

Regarding Jay A. Quealy, Jr., and his services to the Church, Elder Gordon B. Hinckley has said:

> He is a remarkable man. He grew up in an affluent home, the son of a mother who loved the Church and who planted in him a seed of faith which flourished and strengthened through the years. As a young man he was called on a mission to Argentina, where he contracted trichinosis from eating pork and was returned home because of illness. After recuperating his strength he was reassigned to the Northwestern States Mission, where he completed an honorable mission. He then went to Hawaii, where he met the charming girl who became his wife.
>
> He served as bishop and stake president in Hawaii, and then responded without hesitation to go to Hong Kong.
>
> Under his direction the work expanded. He had the vision of the growth of the kingdom through the nations of southeast Asia and constantly expressed the wish that we should be moving out to expand into Malaysia, Indonesia, and India.
>
> It is a miracle that he was not killed in an accident in Hong Kong; and when it was generally felt that he should return home for expert medical care, he insisted on remaining at his post. While still seriously crippled he traveled to Taiwan, the Philippines, and down through southeast Asia to keep the work moving.
>
> The first buildings constructed by the Church in that part of the earth were built during his presidency.

New Presidents and a New Era

When Keith E. Garner of Palo Alto, California, began his three-year assignment as president of the far-flung Southern Far East Mission, the nonmember population was about 1.7 billion, living in Hong Kong, Taiwan, Vietnam, Malaysia (including Singapore), Thailand, and outpost groups as far removed as India. Even to cover the territory of the mission was an almost insuperable responsibility.

With the arrival of President Garner and his family in east Asia on August 13, 1965, extensive work was carried out in organizing and strengthening the auxiliaries and the local membership. The Hong Kong District was divided October 17, 1965, into the Hong Kong and the Kowloon districts, with Malan R. Jackson as president of the former and Ng Kat Hing as president of the latter. On November 20, 1966, C. I. Chan became the first local member to preside over the Hong Kong District.

One of the climactic events in the history of missionary work among the Chinese was the publication of the Book of Mormon in that language. This scripture first became available to the Saints there in December, 1965. Under President Garner's energetic leadership, the Chinese edition of the Book of Mormon became a valuable proselyting tool and an important means for strengthening the faith and understanding of the members as well.

The Taipei chapel in Taiwan was completed and dedicated on October 16, 1966, by Elder Gordon B. Hinckley. This was the first chapel constructed by the Church in the great "Chinese realm" of which President McKay had spoken in his dedicatory prayer in 1921. On that date there were sixteen branches within four districts in Taiwan, where nearly ninety missionaries were laboring. On April 16, 1967, the Un Long chapel of the Hong Kong zone, ground for which had been purchased in June, 1964, was dedicated by President Hugh B. Brown of the First Presidency.

Signs of approaching stability among the Chinese leadership in the Hong Kong-Taiwan areas are revealed in statistics regarding holders of the Melchizedek Priesthood. In late

February, 1968, when Elder Spencer W. Kimball of the Council of the Twelve visited the Asian missions, the Kowloon District had eighty-one Chinese elders, 64 percent of whom were either fully or partly active. Of the total number, however, only 26 percent were married to members of the Church. In the Hong Kong District there were thirty-three elders, making a total of one hundred and fourteen in the Hong Kong zone. Of the thirty-three, 60 percent were participating, among whom 24 percent were married to nonmembers of the Church. In the Taiwan Zone at that time there were ninety-five local elders, about 68 percent of whom were either fully or partially active. Thirty-five percent of this number were married to members of the Church.

Of Keith E. Garner's selection as mission president and of his dedication to the work of the Lord, Brother Hinckley has recalled:

> President Robert Sherman Taylor having faithfully completed the mission for which he had been called, the First Presidency expressed the view that a new president should be found for the Southern Far East Mission. Because of various personal circumstances, all who had been considered were not in a position to go. President Henry D. Moyle had said to me, "We must find someone and do it quickly."
>
> I had been assigned to a stake conference in Utah. At the last minute President Joseph Fielding Smith of the Council of the Twelve changed my assignment to the Palo Alto Stake conference. I did not question why, but simply did as I was told to do. While attending that conference I met for the first time in my life Keith E. Garner, who was on the high council and who had served a mission in Hawaii. I talked with him for a few minutes privately, and he mentioned his mission to Hawaii. I had a very clear and distinct impression that he was the man to preside over the Southern Far East Mission, and I returned and communicated that information to the First Presidency.
>
> He left a thriving business without giving it a second thought except to turn it over to his associates. This was indicative of the spirit of the man. While he presided he gave of his strength and time without any personal consideration, traveling up and down South Vietnam with little regard for his personal safety, being constantly on the move through the vast area of the mission that at that time included Taiwan, the Philippines, Hong Kong, South Vietnam, Thailand, Singapore, and India.
>
> I have never seen a man of his age struggle more diligently to

learn Cantonese, and it was an inspiration to me when I was with him on many occasions to hear him converse in Cantonese.

His able wife was a convert to the Church and this gave her a great appreciation for those who struggled within their hearts to leave that to which they are accustomed and move into a new world as members of the Church.

When W. Brent Hardy was called to preside over the Southern Far East Mission in the summer of 1968, its extent was still unmanageably great. In September, 1969, when it was announced that the new Southeast Asian Mission would be formed from a division of the Southern Far East Mission, and that the latter would be named the Hong Kong-Taiwan Mission, the parent mission had ten districts: two in Hong Kong, three in Taiwan, one each in Thailand and Singapore, and three for servicemen in Vietnam. There was also an amorphous outlying district that included Burma, Indonesia, India, Laos, Malaysia, and Pakistan. At that time President Hardy could report a total of 875 native Melchizedek Priesthood bearers, 2,294 holders of the Aaronic Priesthood, and eleven Church-owned buildings.

IV

JAPAN

JAPAN

President Heber J. Grant has related an impressive experience in connection with his call to open up the Japan Mission. He was in a meeting with the First Presidency and the Council of the Twelve when President George Q. Cannon, one of the counselors in the First Presidency, announced to the brethren, "We are going to open a mission in Japan." Brother Grant said that the impression came to him as plainly as if it had been shouted, "And you are going to be called to that mission." Immediately the thought came into his mind: "My heavens, I certainly cannot afford to go on that mission! I am owing over $100,000, and everything I have in the world would not pay more than $70,000 of it. I will come home $50,000 worse off than nothing. I will tell the brethren I can't do it."

Then "the other Spirit" prompted: "It is marvelous the way the Lord has blessed you; you had better go on that mission." And he said to himself, "O Lord, I acknowledge thy hand in blessing me beyond anything I could have hoped for or expected. I am ready to go, and I shall go without making excuses."

The two spirits continued to strive with him while President Cannon was talking. Finally President Cannon said he understood that Brother Grant was out of all his financial difficulties and was going to celebrate his freedom from debt by making a trip around the world, and that he would stop in Japan.

The thought came to him, "There you are; all you need do is to tell them the true situation and they wouldn't think of sending you on that mission." Again the positive impression came from the other Spirit. "I promised the Lord I will go, and I shall do so."

President Lorenzo Snow asked Brother Grant if he had made the remark about being free from debt and going around the world, and he answered that he had, but there should be one little word added—"if." Brother Grant assured the brethren that he could arrange his affairs so that he could accept the call.

After the meeting, Elder John W. Taylor stopped President Grant and said, "Heber, I know the financial sacrifice you have made this day in accepting this call. I prophesy that you shall be blessed of the Lord and shall make enough money to go to Japan a free man financially. Furthermore, I am inspired to tell you how to do it. You are not to plan to make any money, but you are to get down on your knees every morning and tell the Lord you want to make some money that day, and then go out and get it. You will be astonished how easily you will make the money."

President Grant later related that he went home for his lunch and got down on his knees and thanked the Lord for the prophecy and for the assurance that had come to him that it would be fulfilled. While he was still on his knees, an inspiration came to him regarding the Utah Sugar Company, which resulted in a net gain to him of $30,000.

Without any solicitation on his part, several companies with which he was connected voted to give him a three-year leave of absence with full pay. Within four months, all his financial troubles had disappeared and he was able to go to Japan a free man financially. Thus he consistently maintained that the Lord had commanded him to go to Japan, and that he had prepared a way whereby he might fulfill that assignment.[1]

He had but one charge laid upon his shoulders by the President of the Church, Lorenzo Snow, who at a farewell reception given at the Beehive House on June 26, 1901, remarked:

When the Lord first sent forth his elders in this generation,

[1]Joseph Anderson, "When a Man is Called of God," *The Instructor*, August, 1964.

very little was known as to what their labors would be and what they would accomplish. They failed in some respects, but they did not fail in one thing: they did their duty. As to these brethren who will shortly leave for Japan, the Lord has not revealed to me that they will succeed, but he has shown to me positively that it is their duty to go. They need not worry concerning results, only they should be careful to search the Spirit of the Lord, and understand its language.[2]

Three men and a boy sailed into Tokyo Bay aboard the *Empress of India* early in the morning of August 12, 1901. They were from Utah. Their leader was Heber J. Grant, one of the twelve apostles of the Church. With him were Horace S. Ensign, Louis A. Kelsch, and Alma O. Taylor, age 19. Their arrival marked the beginning of Mormon missionary work in Japan and the establishment of the first Church mission in Asia.

On Sunday morning, September 1, these four elders retired to a wooded area east of Yokohama, and after song and individual supplication, President Grant offered a heartfelt dedicatory prayer. Of that prayer, Elder Taylor wrote:

His tongue was loosened and the Spirit rested mightily upon him; so much so that we felt the angels of God were near; for our hearts burned within us as the words fell from his lips. I never experienced such a peaceful influence or heard such a powerful prayer before. Every word penetrated into my very bones, and I could have wept for joy.

The Japanese islands were dedicated "for the proclamation of the Truth and for the bringing to pass of the purposes of the Lord concerning the gathering of Israel and the establishment of righteousness upon the earth."[3]

Thus began the first Asian mission of the Church. However, despite initial optimism, its results were sporadic and disappointing. Between 1901 and 1924 (when the Japan Mission was closed under instructions of Heber J. Grant, who had become President of the Church), there were seven mission presidents, eighty-eight missionaries, and a total of only 166 baptisms.

[2]*Journal History*, April-June, 1901, pp. 5-6.
[3]See Appendix A, Part II, of Murray L. Nichols, *History of the Japan Mission of The Church of Jesus Christ of Latter-day Saints, 1901-1924*, M.A. Thesis, Brigham Young University, November, 1957.

When Hilton A. Robertson, the last of the mission presidents, was instructed to dispose of Church property and withdraw to Hawaii, there were only about a dozen foreign missionaries in Japan.

The dedication of Japan for the preaching of the gospel, September 1, 1901. Left to right: Horace S. Ensign, Alma O. Taylor, Heber J. Grant of the Council of the Twelve, and Louis A. Kelsch.

A small group of these early Japanese converts were baptized and remained faithful to the Church throughout World War II and until missionaries returned in 1948. But generally the Japanese people were not ready to receive the gospel. The times were out of joint for the Church in Asia. Elbert D. Thomas, mission president between 1910 and 1912, quipped that "instead of thrusting in our sickles, we were swinging our grubbing hoes." Lloyd O. Ivie, mission president between 1921 and 1923, reported that a Utah college professor told him that he had been called to Japan as a youngster before he started college but had refused because "he just couldn't see any future in it." President Grant himself later told President Ivie that before he left Japan the last time, he went out into a grove and prayed for the Lord to send him on a "real mission" when he got home.

During the years of the first Japan Mission, the Japanese

were enthralled with their own rising prospects as a world power and exhilarated by their defeat of China in 1895 and of Russia in 1905. Prejudice against foreigners (particularly Americans) and a new pride in things Japanese were greatly aggravated by the deterioration of Japanese-American relations arising from newly enacted and prejudicial alien exclusion laws in the United States, which were directed against Orientals. The Japanese empire was in a heady mood.

In addition to the harvesting of a few worthy souls and the personal development of the missionaries who labored in Japan during those arduous years, there were two particularly significant developments: (1) Alma O. Taylor completed a translation of the Book of Mormon into Japanese—a memorable accomplishment, and (2) the land of Japan was dedicated and blessed under the authority of the holy apostleship for the reception of the gospel. The sovereign will of the Lord thus began to operate in Japanese affairs to prepare conditions under which "the purposes of the Lord concerning the gathering of Israel and the establishment of righteousness" among the Japanese people might be fulfilled, as invoked by President Grant in his dedicatory prayer.

As early as 1855, in one of the most remarkable prophecies of this dispensation, Elder Parley P. Pratt of the Council of the Twelve wrote that two great enterprises needed to be consummated in order to complete preparations necessary for the fulfillment of the words of the prophets in regard to the restoration of Israel in the last days. First, physically speaking, transcontinental railroads must be built from Europe to Asia and across the North American continent; second, politically speaking,

> some barriers yet remain to be removed, and some conquests to be achieved, such as the subjugation of Japan, and the triumph of constitutional liberty among certain' nations where mind, and thought, and religion are still prescribed by law.[4]

Similar intimations of things to come were expressed by pioneer Mormon missionaries in Japan. Elder Lewis H. Moore

---

[4]Parley P. Pratt, *Key to the Science of Theology* (Liverpool: F. D. Richards, 1855), pp. 73-75.

of Vernal, Utah, had been in the field barely three months when he wrote the following remarkably insightful letter to his family from Sapporo on August 31, 1923:

> We certainly have a mighty big problem to solve over here. This people are certainly a stiff necked bunch. *Something will have to happen to humble them before they will receive the Gospel as they should.* Even our saints, after they have claimed to believe and have been baptized, many of them take it as matter of fact, and quit coming to Church. But there are one or two who are real saints and are willing to work, and do their part. But after considering the time since this mission was established in nineteen one (1901), about twenty three years ago, it almost discourages one. If you convert one member in a family and he comes out to church he never brings any of his brothers or sisters with him. They never talk to anyone else about it to get them to come. So you see we have to meet each individual and labor with him or her personally or we get no results. They just won't think seriously of their religion.
>
> Japan is getting about like Germany was. All they think of is military life. It is taught them from the ground up. All the girls are trained nurses and all the boys trained soldiers. The other day a little boy, probably about ten years of age, was telling his little brother about us. It was at the place where we were boarding in Sapporo. He said, yes we Americans were big, but that we would be like Russia was, we would be easy to whip. So you see that is instilled into them from childhood. It seems that they all expect to fight America sometime. All I can say is that I pray God it never happens. If it does it will be one of the most deadly wars that was ever fought.
>
> The boasting in America about how easy Japan could be licked would be hushed if they could just spend some time here and see that these people would be forces to be feared. They are marvelously skilled in hand to hand fighting. They are good shots, they are hardy, and coupled with this they have that utter disregard for life. They think it a great glory to die in a fight. I would pity the man who encountered a Japanese in a hand to hand fight. They are as strong as bulls, and athletic and very quick. I sincerely hope that we never clash with them. *But something is going to cause their downfall, of that I am certain. It's in the air so to speak. They are getting all together too proud, and ambitious. And when the fall comes it will be a hard one. It will have to almost wipe them off the earth in order to break their pride.* (Italics by the author.)

The day after this letter was written, Japan suffered the greatest earthquake of all time. The great cities of Tokyo and Yokohama were flattened and practically destroyed through great conflagrations that ensued. By the time the fires were brought under control (which took many days), three-quarters of Tokyo and four-fifths of Yokohama had been destroyed. Tokyo's list of dead and missing amounted to 107,000 and Yokohama's to 33,000, most of them victims of what Tokyo's residents, who have suffered from them ever since their city was known as Edo, cynically called *Edo no hana*—the Flowers of Edo: fires.

Significant among Church happenings in Japan at this time was the visit of David O. McKay, then an apostle. The following account is taken from Hugh J. Cannon's narrative already quoted concerning China:

Elders McKay and Cannon in Japan

The Japanese mission, at the time of President McKay's visit in 1921, was in charge of President Joseph H. Stimpson, then nearing the end of his second term of service there, he having spent a total of eleven years in that field. His wife had accompanied him as a bride on the last mission and at the time of this visit they had three beautiful children, the oldest of which talked Japanese as fluently as he did English. Perhaps no better opportunity will present itself to say that Sister Stimpson is one of the gems of the Church, hospitable, industrious and willing to expatriate herself because of her deep and abiding love for missionary work.

The Mission Home was a comfortable one. Conforming to usual Japanese custom, the visitors were immediately invited to bathe, and having heard of the novel methods, they were glad to accept. A fire is built in the iron box in one end of the tub, which in this instance was a wooden affair about four feet deep and nearly as wide. This oven heats the water almost to the boiling point. The bather is supposed to wash himself thoroughly, for which purpose there is a basin, soap, and hose with running water; then he climbs into the tub and soaks in water as hot as it is humanly possible to have it and live. Thus the entire family bathes in the same water without having it become very dirty.

Under President Stimpson's direction an interesting Christmas program was given at the home. The natives sat on mats on the floor with feet doubled up under them for nearly three hours and apparently enjoyed it.

Meetings were attended by the special missionaries in Tokyo, Kofu and in Osaka. The people listen attentively, but it is rather discouraging to think that after almost twenty years of earnest work there are only 125 Church members in Japan. Brother McKay intended going to Hokkaido on the north island, where there was a branch of the Church. A start was made, with Brother and Sister Stimpson and their baby in the party. The steamer, plying between islands, was anchored in the open sea and a tug conveyed the passengers to it. A violent storm was raging, and even before the tug left its pier it began bucking after the fashion of a western bronco. Passengers resembled animated shuttle-cocks. Sister Stimpson literally tossed her baby to Brother Cannon while she threw sundry other things to the fishes. This was her first experience with the malady. As the tug came alongside the steamer, the danger of attempting to jump from one vessel to the other became evident. One moment they would crash violently together and the next would be so far apart that even a trained broad jumper could not make the spring. A strong impression to turn back came to Brother McKay, and though greatly disappointed all agreed it would be unwise to proceed in face of his feeling.

David O. McKay (center) and companion Hugh J. Cannon (third from right) with Japanese members and missionaries in 1921: Tsune Nachie, far left, who did the first temple work for the Saints of Japan in the Hawaiian temple; and Elders Deloss Watson Holley (left of Elder McKay) and Howard Jenson (between McKay and Cannon).

The suitcases, etc., were being shifted to the steamer when President Stimpson's attention was called to the fact that he was losing his luggage.

He turned, and his face, a pitiful-mixture of ashy gray and yellow-ish green, confirmed his words: "My luggage isn't the only thing I'm losing."

It should be recorded to Brother McKay's credit that in this in-cident he escaped sea-sickness by an extremely narrow margin.

It will never be known what would have occurred had they gone on, but having in mind the prophetic words that the head of this tour should be inspired to avoid dangers seen and unseen, no one would have dared disregard the impression.

The Japanese are as modest as the Yankees, and not a whit more so, when talking of their own land. One is not justified in speaking of the beautiful, they say, until Nikko has been seen. It is truly a delightful place and a visit there vindicates in large measure the pride which the natives have in it. The ornate temples and "sacred" places are bewildering in number and beauty, though some of the beauty borders on the grotesque. Indeed, throughout Japan there is a mixture of the sublime and what to a European is the ridiculous, how sublime and how ridiculous only those know who have visited the land.

At all sacred places the visitors had to remove their shoes, and at the "Sanctum Sanctorum" they were obliged to discard overcoats as well, despite extremely cold weather.

President Stimpson tells of three elders who visited this place and were told at the door that no one without faith could enter.

"We have faith," was the missionary's reply.

"If you have faith, you may come in for one yen each."

"But we have more faith than that," replied the Elder. "We have faith that we can all come in for one yen." Their faith was effective.

One's stock of adjectives is exhausted in attempting to describe the carvings and decorations on the buildings. Here are the originals of the three monkeys, one of which holds his hand over eyes, one over mouth and one ears, indicating that man should see no evil, speak no evil and hear no evil. The cryptomeria trees are as indescribable as the temples. They are extremely tall and stately evergreens, many of them six or seven feet in diameter and some of them much more than that.

At one place many stone lanterns about six feet high were seen, and among them was one which according to tradition had formed the intolerable habit of turning into a ghost and frightening everybody away, so a wire cage was placed around it. Since then it has behaved properly.

After viewing the river, the waterfalls, forests, temples and shrines we left the place with the feeling that the Japanese are not far wrong in their boastful statement regarding its beauty.

In the car with Brother McKay and his party between Nikko and Tokyo were a number of natives. In one corner was a dainty young lady attired in the usual attractive Japanese style, with elaborate hair dressing, highly colored and beautiful kimono, stockings which reached to her ankles and the inevitable wooden sandals. She was accompanied by a young man and older lady, and in due time they opened a package of lunch. Chop sticks, kept in sealed wax paper, as a sanitary measure, were used to pick up the food, not a particle of which was touched by the hands. The skill displayed in using these sticks attracted the attention of our curious Americans and perhaps they watched the diners more intently than good breeding would permit. Finally, the lunch reminded them that thoughtful Sister Stimpson had brought along a box of sandwiches and they too began their meal.

Think about how an American eats a sandwich! He takes it in one hand, or perhaps two, and tears away at it very much as a bear would do. It was not long until, instead of being observers, the Americans became the observed. A little girl sitting opposite tried vainly not to smile. Too polite to laugh openly, she turned her head and looked out the window to conceal her amusement.

The missionaries believed their hands were clean at the commencement of the meal, but at its conclusion Brother McKay went to the washroom, and when he rejoined the party, remarked: "Do you know what those people said as I came by them? If they did not actually say it they thought, 'Now that he has eaten with his dirty hands he has washed them.' "

After all, many habits which seem peculiar or even ridiculous to us might be imitated with profit.

If evidence of the divinity of this work were needed, it could be found in the love which characterizes the missionary. With possibly one exception, the visitors had met none of these brethren before; but still they seemed to be life-long acquaintances—nay, more than that, of one family, brothers in the flesh instead of merely in belief. As the visiting party boarded the train for Osaka, the elders remaining in Tokyo ran along the platform again to press Brother McKay's hand and hear his words, "The Lord bless you, my brother."

Nara, former capital of the empire, is not far behind Nikko as a show place. Its artistic park is full of deer, believed by the Japanese to be sacred. They will eat from a stranger's hand. There was a sacred horse, which, probably due to ignorance on the subject, looked like a common glasseyed cayuse. There were sacred pigeons, temples and bells. It would appear that nearly everything is sacred to a Japanese except his promise, but unless he is outrageously maligned he esteems a promise as the least sacred thing in the world.

Fourteen hours with an express train carried the travelers from Osaka to Shimonoseki, the point of embarkation for Fusan, in Korea. As they proceeded southward the climate became milder and before the sea was reached many heavily laden orange trees were seen. Men and women were plowing their rice fields, if drawing a pointed stick to which a cow is hitched, through mud almost knee deep, can be called plowing.

Comfortable quarters were obtained aboard the *Komo Maru,* which plies between this Japanese island and the mainland of Asia. As the vessel left the busy and lighted harbor and entered the inky blackness which prevailed outside and the brethren thought of the strange country and people to which they were going, their own ignorance of the customs and language, they thought of another journey taken by a man oppressed with serious sickness and the exalted words which he wrote:

"Lead, kindly light, amid the encircling gloom,
Lead Thou me on!
The night is dark, and I am far from home;
Lead Thou me on!
Keep Thou my feet; I do not ask to see
The distant scene; one step enough for me."

The Japan Mission After World War II

Early in 1937 the Japan Mission was reopened with head-quarters in Honolulu, Hawaii, and Hilton Robertson was named president. Missionary work was confined to Japanese living in Hawaii, but President Robertson made several trips to Japan. However, it was only in the aftermath of a great and painful war in which the Japanese had been profoundly shaken by their first national defeat, and in which they were disillusioned with many of the myths of their own past, that they became receptive to the gospel message.

Edward L. Clissold was appointed to preside over the newly rejuvenated Japan Mission in October 1947, but it was not until early 1948 that he was able to gain permission from the United States War Department to enter Japan and reestablish Church work there. By that time Mormon service-men had already began their own kind of missionary work among the Japanese.

At first, the Japanese people faced the American occupa-tion forces with mixed feelings of wonder and fear, but those foreign soldiers were generally amiable and generous. Latter-day Saint GI's in particular radiated the gospel through the power of their example, and Japanese were drawn to them. The story of Tatsui Sato of Narumi village is a case in point. His conversion story, as impressively recounted by Harrison T. Price in 1962[5], is typical of the workings of the Lord in post-war Asia:

Foreign soldiers came to his village to trade items of food for silk and curios. It was then that a knowledge of English became the most valuable talent in the hungry village, and the merchants suddenly recalled a man who understood such a strange tongue. In the past some had ridiculed this quiet, scholarly man for his strong faith in the Christian Bible, but Tatsui Sato was now a voice for the village.

November 22, 1945, was cold and quiet as Sato San discussed the hard times with villagers gathered in a tea shop near the North Bridge. It was almost dark when someone

---

[5]Harrison T. Price, "A Cup of Tea," *The Improvement Era*, Vol. 65, March 1962, pp. 160ff.

Sister T. Kumagai of Sapporo, Japan, one of the few early Japanese converts who remained faithful during World War II.

Elder Matthew Cowley and Edward L. Clissold after the reopening of Japan, meeting here with three Japanese Saints: Tsurichi Katsura, Eiko Nagao, and Dr. Hisada.

noticed three American soldiers standing in the deserted road outside. They appeared to be waiting for a ride to a military camp. Through the windows of the shop, the foreigners could be seen stamping their feet on the hard ground outside to keep warm, as their breath showed in the frosty air. Several people suggested inviting them into the shop to warm themselves, but only Sato San could speak English.

The three foreign soldiers looked up in surprise as the dignified Japanese man asked in English: "Won't you come in and get warm while you are waiting?" Sato San then recognized one of the men as a Mr. Mel Arnold, who had previously come to his silk and curio store. The other two men introduced themselves as Ray Hanks and Reed Davis.

Inside the shop the Americans expressed their thanks as they rubbed their hands over the meager coals in the hibachi charcoal brazier. As a token of hospitality, the master of the house presented each visitor with a hot boiled chicken egg to warm the hands and stomach. When a woman brought steaming cups of the best Shizuoka green tea, however, the villagers were astonished to see the foreigners decline to drink it. "Thank you, but we do not drink tea or use other stimulants," Hanks said. "Our church teaches us that our bodies are a very sacred gift from God, and that we should take special care of our health."

"This is a very strange teaching," Sato San said. "I have never heard of such a belief, although I have studied the Bible."

The visitors then explained about a revelation from God called the Word of Wisdom, and also said that the believers in this church were called Mormons after a sacred history book copied from ancient records. In answer to his request, one of the Americans promised to bring Sato San a copy of this Book of Mormon when they came again. As the three men left to board a big truck, one villager was heard to say, "*Mezurashii Ne*—these Americans are very strange indeed. I'm afraid that they cannot be understood like ordinary people."

As promised, Mel Arnold and Ray Hanks did return to Narumi with a Book of Mormon, and began to hold study classes with the Sato family. Tatsui Sato read the book carefully from cover to cover and then reread, studied, and prayed. Other Mormon soldiers came to their small home now, and Sato San and his wife started a small Sunday School for neighborhood children. Later they began inviting Japanese friends to the weekly study classes. On the night of January 27, 1946, a young Mormon chaplain, Norton Nelson, came to their gospel study class during a blinding snowstorm. After the closing prayer that night, a full moon broke through the clouds to reveal a glittering landscape of deep new snow. The storm had completely stopped all road traffic. Chaplain Nelson and his friends waded through the snow all that night to return the thirty miles to their replacement depot near the town of Okazaki.

There was sickness in the Sato family, but the new friends brought candies and foreign foods. For the first time in his life Sato's young son, Yasuo, tasted various strange canned fruits and meats. One unnamed Mormon serviceman may have helped save their lives during this hungry post-war period. Each day for several months he stopped his big Army bread truck at the North Bridge just long enough to throw down several loaves of still warm GI bread. There were many prayers of thanks each time as he roared off down the dusty road again.

By the time the summer rains came to Narumi village, Tatsui Sato and his wife Chiyo were convinced that the Book of Mormon was true. Their lives had changed greatly since the Latter-day Saint servicemen had first declined to drink their tea and had told of their beliefs. On July 7, 1946, Tatsui Sato was baptized in a swimming pool at Kansai University in Osaka by C. Elliot Richards. Tatsui's faithful wife, Chiyo, and young son Yasuo were also baptized and confirmed that day. Sister Sato was baptized by Boyd K. Packer, who later became one of the twelve apostles of the Church. This was the first baptism of local Saints in Japan in over twenty years and the beginning of a new era for the Church in the Far East.

As the postwar missionary work spread out among the ninety million people of Japan, Brother and Sister Tatsui Sato were among the many who helped open the way. Many who later joined the Church were to first hear the inspiring Joseph Smith story while seated on the *tatami* straw mats in the little Sato home. Over the years numerous new elders came to an understanding of the complex Japanese language through the patient explanations of Brother Sato.

On June 12, 1949, Elder Matthew Cowley ordained Brother Sato an elder. This was the first such ordination to the Melchizedek Priesthood in Japan in several decades.

Vinal G. Mauss, a well-known Oakland, California, businessman, was called to succeed Edward L. Clissold as president of the Japan Mission. During his presidency important building sites were purchased in Tokyo and Yokohama, and missionaries were sent out to open up new proselyting areas in the country. President Mauss characterized the progress of the mission and the trend of the times in this report:

> There has been a splendid response from the members in living the principles of the gospel. It has been most gratifying to see them change their ways and customs in keeping the Sabbath day holy and attending their church services. There have been several reports where young members have been instrumental in

President and Sister Vinal G. Mauss, who were in Japan between 1949 and 1952.

getting their parents to stop the age-old custom of drinking tea in the home. . . . With the expected peace treaty coming into effect it is generally felt there will naturally be considerable adjusting and a period of leveling off which may bring some difficulties. The past year has been a prosperous year for Japan as a whole and we have noticed it in the attitude of the people. There has developed the spirit of indifference which always seems to come when there is an abundance of material things.[6]

Between 1955 and 1962 there was a great surge of baptisms in the Northern Far East Mission: 141 in 1955; 386 in 1956; 638 in 1957; 735 in 1958; 596 in 1959; 927 in 1960; 1,290 in 1961; and 1,603 in 1962.

Elder Cowley, as supervisor of Pacific and Oriental missions, in September, 1949, reflected on the dramatic post-war changes in Japan:

In Japan we have one of the greatest opportunities for missionary service I have ever heard of or read in the history of the Church. . . . We have a marvelous opportunity there. The people will join the Church there if we give them the missionaries. They want to know the gospel.[7]

In 1902 Elder Charles W. Penrose of the Council of the Twelve, in commenting on the opening of missionary work in Japan, anticipated the future of the Church in East Asia with remarkable accuracy when he declared that Japan would be an effectual doorway through which the gospel would be taken to other countries in Asia:

We shall find, I believe with all my heart, that the opening of the Japanese Mission will prove the key to the entrance of the gospel to the Orient. We will find that an influence will go out from Japan into other Oriental nations. The ice has been broken and the barriers will be removed from the way and the gospel will spread into other eastern nations.[8]

When this statement was made, Church prospects in Japan had few encouraging signs. Subsequent labors in the 1920s did little to change the dismal picture. But now with hindsight,

---

[6]Vinal G. Mauss, "Report of the Mission President," *Mission Annual Reports,* 1951, p. 281.

[7]Matthew Cowley, "The Language of Sincerity," *The Improvement Era,* November 1949, p. 715.

[8]Charles W. Penrose, *Conference Report,* April 6, 1902, p. 52.

and especially since the developments of World War II, one can see that out of those simple beginnings great things have been brought to pass, not only vindicating what Alma taught, that "by very small means the Lord doth confound the wise and bringeth about the salvation of many souls" (Alma 37:6-7), but also lending zest to Joseph F. Smith's prophetic promise, given when Elder Grant first set forth on his mission to Japan:

> We expect Brother Grant to do his duty in that calling, and and we know he will, and we will sustain him by our faith and prayers. I do not care whether he succeeds in learning the language or not, if he will stay there until the servants of God say, "Come home," his name will go down to all time in honor and blessing, and hundreds, yea thousands and perhaps millions, will receive the Gospel as a result of his labors in the beginning.[9]

And thus it has come to pass. Japan has become a lodestar of the fledgling Asian missions of the Church.

Okinawa

The work of the Church was also extended to the Ryukyu Islands during these years of expansion. These islands were dedicated for the preaching of the gospel by President Joseph Fielding Smith on Sunday, August 14, 1955. At that time the servicemen were instructed to begin negotiations for the purchase of a chapel site. Later that year a chapel site was purchased near the town of Futenma. By April, 1956, the land had been leveled, a quonset building donated by the U.S. Army had been moved onto the land, and initial plans for a new chapel had been approved by the First Presidency.

Prior to the arrival of the missionaries, three Okinawans were baptized into the Church by the servicemen: Sisters Nobu Nakamura, Ayako Nakamura, and Kuniko Tamanaha. They were baptized in the East China Sea on Christmas Day, 1955.

The first full-time elders arrived in Naha on Tuesday morning, April 17, 1956, aboard the *Hakusan Maru*. These missionaries—Clarence LeRoy B. Anderson, president of the newly formed Okinawa district of the Northern Far East Mis-

---

[9]Quoted in Preston Nibley, *The Presidents of the Church* (Salt Lake City: Deseret Book Company, 1959), p. 299.

sion, and his companion, Sam K. Shimabukuro—were met at the pier by several Latter-day Saint servicemen and wives who took them to the home of Sister Nobu Nakamura, where they lived until quarters were found.

As with the opening of all new areas of labor in the expanding Asian missions, living conditions for the pioneer elders in Okinawa were humble and inconvenient. President Paul C. Andrus reported on December 17, 1956:

> The missionaries are now living in the quonset hut on the Church property, even though they do not yet have water. All their water is carried to them in five gallon cans by members of the Church who are in the armed services. Brother Lew Cramer, Servicemen's District Clerk, has been very faithful in this burdensome task.

Many important Church developments in Northeast Asia came between 1955 and 1962, the period of service of President Andrus, of whom Brother Hinckley has said:

> My first meeting with Paul C. Andrus occurred on my first visit to the Orient. I arrived at night, and he met me at Haneda International Airport. We drove to the mission home through the darkened streets of Tokyo in the old Pontiac station wagon that had been taken there by President Hilton A. Robertson. I followed his example in entering the home in taking off my shoes. This in itself was an introduction to life in the Orient.
> During the succeeding years of his presidency I was with him on many occasions and in many areas. He served altogether a period of six years in addition to three years of service previously as a missionary, making a total of nine years of missionary service in the Orient. During his presidency tremendous strides were made in the work, and the mission reached a maturity that was an inspiration to behold. He and his accomplished wife, who also previously had served as a missionary in Japan, were examples of industry and faithfulness before the members and the missionaries. I have never seen more energetic workers. At the time, the mission included all of Japan, Okinawa, and Korea. They never neglected their children, but somehow notwithstanding they seemed always to be on the move, encouraging the saints and standing as examples before the missionaries. They both spoke Japanese without hesitation and became examples of dedicated service and were an inspiration to all.

If Paul Andrus became known for his pioneering efforts to plant the gospel in a far-flung field, his successors, Dwayne

Elder and Sister Spencer W. Kimball visit President and Sister Adney Y. Komatsu in Tokyo in February, 1968. President Komatsu was the first person of Asian ancestry to preside over a mission of the Church.

Servicemen's conference in Tokyo, November, 1962. Elder Gordon B. Hinckley, third from left; Sister Hinckley, President and Mrs. Dwayne N. Anderson, and Lt. Col. Lewis S. Franck, Far East Servicemen's coordinator.

N. Anderson and Adney Y. Komatsu, should be especially remembered for strengthening the members, building leadership, and establishing the programs of the Church on a firm basis in Japan. In recognition of their labor, of which Project Temple is the best-known example, Brother Hinckley has said the following:

> Dwayne N. Anderson was one of those faithful and devoted seventies who, during a period of war when the Church could not send out young men, responded to a call to full-time missionary service though married and with the responsibilities of a family. He was sent to Hawaii, and his wife Peggy kept him in the field at great personal sacrifice. He later served as a bishop where he did an unusual work in teaching men of the adult Aaronic Priesthood group the gospel and preparing them to go to the temple.
>
> When he was called to preside over the Northern Far East Mission I told him on one occasion in Tokyo that he had a special responsibility to teach leadership to the Japanese brethren, that we were getting converts, but that we were not developing leaders.
>
> He took this responsibility very seriously and did a remarkable work in training local leaders. This effort has flourished and blossomed in a marvelous manner as is evidenced by the strength of our local leaders in Japan today.
>
> There is a thing of significance in the fact that Dwayne Anderson was wounded as an American soldier on the Shuri Line in Okinawa where there were 12,000 American casualties. That bitter experience ripened into a great love as I saw in a very personal way when he and I worked in securing the building site on which today the beautiful chapel in Naha stands, not far from the Shuri Line.
>
> In all of his activities he evidenced that love which comes of a testimony of the reality and divinity of the Prince of Peace.

Regarding Adney Yoshio Komatsu, Brother Hinckley has said:

> How Sister Hinckley and I appreciated the Komatsus. This delightful couple would warm the hearts of anyone who knew them. They represented Japanese Americans at their very best. Both were born in Hawaii. He joined the Church through playing ball with the missionaries, and he brought her into the Church. They were the first of Oriental stock to preside in that part of the earth, and how the Japanese saints loved them. They were likewise loved by the missionaries, who saw in them wonderful examples of what the gospel would do for all Japanese who would accept it. They have won an undying place in the hearts of the people among whom they served so faithfully.

Japan Mission Divided

With the release of President Komatsu on September 1, 1968, and no doubt in part resulting from the great expansion of the Japanese Mission under his leadership, two new missions were formed. Edward Y. Okazaki of Denver, Colorado, was called to preside over the new Japan-Okinawa Mission, and Walter R. Bills, a former Japanese missionary, was placed in charge of the Japan Mission.

"Project Temple"—The Initial Effort

The spirit of Elijah—involving deep concern for the salvation of the dead—moves deeply among the people of Asia. The hearts of the children have been turned toward their parents for many generations. Responsive to Confucian teachings, and no doubt the benign influence of the Lord, that serving those now dead as if they were living is a lofty human achievement, the Asian people have had concern for their ancestors as a basic feature of their life. It has been the very heart of religious faith. Francis Xavier, the famous sixteenth century Catholic missionary, in recognition of this national trait among the Japanese, once lamented:

> There is one tragedy about Japanese followers. That is, they mourn so much over a certain doctrine we teach, namely, the people who have fallen to hell can be saved by no means. It is such a pity to see these people sad, for their love towards deceased parents, wives and children is so great.[10]

Influenced by this background of deep commitment to family and forebears, Asian converts to the Church have proven extraordinarily prepared to understand and appreciate the importance of work for the dead as carried out in the temples of the Lord.

In Japan, where the members have been particularly enthusiastic in their response to genealogy and temple work, the story has been instructive and inspiring. It begins with Lloyd O. Ivie, who succeeded Joseph Stimpson as president of the mission in February, 1921. It includes Sister Nachie, who had been

---

[10]Kenkichi Yamamoto, *Kirishitan Jidai no Senkyoshi* (*Missionaries of the Chistian Era*), Tokyo: Hobunkan.

working in the mission home almost from the beginning, and who was a very faithful and dependable lady. President McKay, after meeting her, had said, "Surely the blood of Israel is here." At that time her daughter, Ei-san (known to the missionaries as Nagao Oba-san, was getting married, so a maid to help Sister Nachie was employed. Not long after that Sister Nachie suggested that she discontinue her employment and go live with a relative.

It was at this juncture that the idea was born of sending her to Hawaii to the temple. She had known all the missionaries from the beginning. They all loved her. During the winter of 1922-23, President Ivie wrote all of the returned missionaries, asking for financial support in sending Sister Nachie to the Hawaii Temple.

By spring, when all else was in readiness, Sister Nachie came to President Ivie with a sad countenance, saying that the *Gaimucho* (Department of the Exterior) had turned down her application for travel abroad. She would not be able to go to Hawaii. President Ivie took her rejection notice along with other papers she had accumulated and, accompanied by Elder Milton B. Taylor, went to the *Gaimucho* in Marunouchi, where he was directed to a small cubbyhole desk at the end of a long corridor. The official was kind and courteous. He referred the Americans to the "gentlemen's agreement" between Japan and the United States, which allowed no laborers to enter America. In answering the question "What will you do for a living," Nachie-san had written "work." She aimed to find employment.

It took some time to explain that such was not the case. Brother Ivie explained that Sister Nachie had served more than twenty years in the mission home of the Church in Japan, during which time many missionaries had come and gone. She had been like a mother to them, and they were contributing the necessary funds. "But," President Ivie argued, "you know the Japanese *dokuritsu-shin* (independent spirit), and how you can detest the very thought of becoming a *yakkai-mono* (parasite on others). As a reward for her faithfulness, the missionaries will take care of her."

This brought from the official the only response he could give. Her statement was on the document, so he could do nothing about it. Brother Ivie made another approach. "There is also the matter of her faith. She is very devout. Her religion means everything. Her purpose in going is to perform important temple rituals for herself and her kindred dead." The thought had come to the mission president that every Japanese wishes to make one trip in his lifetime to the great temple at Ise, the national shrine.

This the official understood. He paused for a moment and said, "Write up a new application, explaining the situation as you now have to me, and we will reconsider the application."

In a few days the passport came through. Nachie-san was immediately booked on the *Taiyo Maru,* the next available ship for Hawaii and the largest Japanese passenger ship afloat at that time. (Originally it had been a German ship called the *Emden,* which became a war prize in the South Pacific, a real palace afloat.)

During the time Sister Nachie had been working on her passport, President Ivie went to all the districts of the mission, visited every available member, explained temple work to them, and gathered as many names for temple work as possible. With Japan's traditional concern for ancestor worship, this was not difficult. The members responded enthusiastically. Thus, besides the names Nachie-san had gathered on her own line, more than a hundred other names were obtained.

Sister Nachi returned to Japan at once from Hawaii to get more names. What she accomplished in this pioneering effort in Hawaii, where she finally passed away and is buried, was by no means small or insignificant. Her labor in the temple must be remembered as a crowning achievement of the so-called Old Japan Mission. President Ivie concluded (in April, 1966):

> Thus in a sense, the Old Mission was never closed, but transferred to the other side. We teach the doctrine that in temple work the living can serve the dead. No doubt it works both ways. If spirits could prepare to come to this earth there may be things the dead can do for us. Elijah came to turn the hearts both ways. It is significant that Japan is with us today. . . .

On my return to America in 1924 we stopped at Honolulu for a day. President Neff took us by car to Laie, and President Waddoups showed us the temple. There I met Nachie-san for the last time. She was so full of the missionary spirit that the narration of her experiences had to be cut short in order for us to get back in time for the boat. No greater soul ever lived than she and temple work among the Japanese will ultimately bring salvation to millions, and the Rising Sun will shine again in the light of the gospel.

Project Temple—Stability and a Tokyo Stake

In July, 1965, a group of 166 Japanese members of the Church made a history-making excursion to the Hawaii Temple. This was the first time Oriental Saints were given an opportunity to enter the temple and participate in its sacred rites for themselves and their dead in their own language. The 7,000-mile round-trip journey marked an epoch in the history of the Church.

The successful completion of "Project Temple" was a credit to Japan Mission President Dwayne C. Anderson, who conceived it, and to the 131 adults and twenty-nine children who worked so hard to make it possible. But it actually began in the summer of 1963, when a new Japanese convert named Kenge Yamanaka, a man of considerable standing in Japanese society, was baptized into the Church.

A few months after his baptism, Brother Yamanaka was working as an interpreter and guide for a group of American college professors from California who were in Japan to study. In this group was a lady member of the Church who was married to one of the professors. When she and Brother Yamanaka discovered they were both Latter-day Saints, they spent much time together discussing the Church. She suggested that since he had previously taken tour groups to the United States, he should lead a group of Japanese Saints to Salt Lake City to learn more about the Church. He became very enthusiastic about the idea, but the members in Japan were generally young and not well situated financially. Brother Yamanaka considered ways to raise money to offset this disadvantage. He investigated the costs of flights to the United States, then conferred with President Anderson. He sought permission to take 30 Japanese

Saints on a visit to Church headquarters at Salt Lake City, but in this relatively modest suggestion the mission president saw the potential of something far greater. He visualized Project Temple. President Anderson later reported that he felt inspired to lay plans for a Japanese excursion to the House of the Lord as an initial step toward building a greater sense of Mormon family life and eventual stakehood in Japan.

Project Temple was marked by difficulty, sacrifice, disappointments, faith, and ultimate success. At the outset it was determined that thirty mission, district, and branch leaders would be selected to raise money by projects, and that the mission would supplement these funds to the extent necessary. It was calculated that these leaders would have to raise approximately $4,000. Brother Yamanaka suggested selling pearls and phonograph records of Japanese Latter-day Saint hymns. When the members were consulted, they were enthusiastic but doubted that sufficient money could be raised.

A mission survey was taken to determine how many couples could raise approximately $400 or $500 in a period of eighteen months. The response was excellent. Thus the mission leaders determined that they could charter an entire plane rather than simply make arrangements for a tour of thirty. Application was made to Civil Aeronautics Board in Japan for the right to charter Flying Tigers, who had offered a bid of $300 per seat round trip, but since this airline was a foreign firm,· the government would not allow it to fly in and take Japanese nationals out, so the mission request was denied. Eleven other airlines gave quotations, but all were above $300 per seat, the amount set as the absolute maximum limit.

It was during this time that a serviceman member of the Church, Colonel Robert David, made a trip to Hawaii on temporary duty. While in Hawaii he attended a banquet at which he sat across from a Japan Air Lines representative. They discussed the possibilities of chartered Japan Air Lines flights from Japan to Hawaii. This gentleman told Brother David to come to his office the next day and he would make a bid for such a flight. The bid: $273 per seat round trip.

President Anderson, after being informed of this bid, took

it to the vice-president in charge of sales at JAL in Tokyo. Handing him the letter from the Honolulu executive, President Anderson said, "If you will honor this written bid, we would like to do business with you." The man looked at it and said, "It is official. We will have to honor it." Previously the lowest offer from Japan Air Lines had been $330 per seat round trip.

It was now concluded that the cost to members would be $500 per couple plus their expenses in Hawaii, an extra $100. This would be about one-half of one year's salary per family. These Saints did not own homes or cars or other things they could sell. Most of them would have to simply cut down on food and do without other things to raise the necessary funds. Another problem was that they had never before participated in fund-raising projects, so they had to be taught how to raise funds by such a method. The older members particularly had to be convinced that the idea of fund raising was honorable and Christian.

Procedure was patterned after common practices of the Church in America: merchandise was purchased wholesale, then members (including missionaries, former missionaries, and overseas friends) were asked to pay a given amount for it.

Meanwhile, a list of those planning to participate in Project Temple was compiled. Each individual member was interviewed three times by a member of the mission presidency, not only to determine the member's worthiness but also to keep abreast of his preparations to meet the financial requirement. Information on temples and temple work was compiled into book form, translated into the Japanese language, then used as a course of study for more than a year as part of the home evening lessons.

To further prepare the Japanese Saints for their momentous trip, it was requested that each one prepare and submit three family group sheets, so they would have sufficient names to do work for when they arrived at the Hawaii Temple.

When President McKay learned that the Japanese Saints were earnestly engaged in reaching their goal of entering the temple in Hawaii, he authorized that a translator be sent to Hawaii in order to have the ceremony translated into Japanese.

Brother Sato, a veteran Church translator, spent six months preparing tapes so that the ceremony could be carried out in Japanese.

The Saints arrived in Hawaii in late July, 1965. At that time a round trip airplane ticket from Japan to Hawaii was $621, but through the help of the Lord, this group traveled round trip for $273 per person.

The Japanese visitors were met at the airport in Honolulu by a large group of Hawaiian Saints and were given the traditional welcome consisting of dancing and leis. It was an impressive welcome with many tears flowing and marked by an array of brilliantly colored, flowing muumuus and aloha shirts. On hand also to greet the Japanese Saints were local Church leaders headed by President Edward L. Clissold of the Hawaii Temple, President George W. Poulsen, Jr., of the Hawaii Mission, and President Paul C. Andrus, former mission president in Japan. Elder Gordon B. Hinckley, supervisor of Hawaii-Oriental missions of the Church at the time, who was also in attendance, commented that "the tremendous greeting given the Japanese Saints by the Hawaiian Saints who welcomed them at the airport is an evidence of the power of the gospel in creating a spirit of love among people of various lands."[11]

The visitors were housed at the student dormitories of the Church College of Hawaii, but they spent at least one home evening in the homes of the members of the Oahu Stake. They were thus able to gain firsthand experience in Mormon homes in an established stake of Zion. In the Oahu Stake, leaders were given opportunity to attend leadership meetings corresponding to those of their own positions in Japan. Branch presidents attended meetings with bishoprics throughout Sunday so they were able to see the functioning of organized wards and an established stake. Another purpose of the trip was to obtain patriarchal blessings. All patriarchs in Hawaii were kept busy giving blessings during the time the Japanese Saints were there.

In the Temple

President Clissold of the Hawaii Temple observed that in

[11]*Church News,* July 31, 1965, p. 3.

preparing the Japanese members for the temple service, he had never known of a people better prepared spiritually than that first group of Oriental saints. Not only had they made all of their own temple clothing before they arrived, but they were also fully prepared in every way to participate in ordinances for the living and the dead. The meeting held just before the first session began, according to all accounts, was one of the most inspiring meetings ever held in the Hawaii Temple.

The Japanese members reportedly felt so much at home in the temple that they simply did not want to leave. Many tears of joy were shed. Such powerful feelings are unusual for the Japanese people, who are not characteristically an emotional people. Of course, their tears were understandable. Temple work for departed ancestors was a particular source of joy for them.

President Anderson returned to Japan after the temple sessions were completed. What a wonderful culmination of his service as mission president! Adney Y. Komatsu was then called to lead missionary work in Japan. President Komatsu furthered the cause begun by President Anderson, and a second excursion to Hawaii was made in 1967. Approximately twenty of those who had participated in the first trip returned. A third excursion was made in July, 1969.

Project Temple in Japan has encouraged the members of the Church in other parts of Asia. The Saints in Hong Kong and the Philippines have begun to lay plans for excursions of their own. Under the guidance of President Robert H. Slover, and with the help and sacrifice of members, servicemen, and returned missionaries, five members of the Korean Mission were able to lay plans for the first excursion from that mission to the Hawaii Temple, with a stop en route at the Mormon Pavilion at Expo '70 in Osaka.

Project Temple has significantly changed the outlook of the Japanese Saints toward themselves and their church. Their devotion has been strengthened because they have been able to see how the gospel relates itself to their families and other patterns long accepted in their own tradition. Another benefit was indicated by Elder Gordon B. Hinckley, who said in 1968 that "there is now the potential for a stake in Japan." Activities surrounding Project Temple have undoubtedly been a major impetus in preparing such leadership.

A Temple in Japan

In July, 1949, Elder Matthew Cowley of the Council of Twelve, while offering the dedicatory prayer for the newly acquired mission home in Tokyo, uttered a prophetic promise: "There will some day be many Church buildings, and even temples in this land."[12] In view of the precarious condition of the Church in Asia at that time, this was a truly breathtaking prediction. But in view of subsequent events, the growth of the Church in East Asia, and especially the mounting tide of interest in temple work among the Saints in that part of the world, today it seems almost within reach of fulfillment. The expanding interest and activity in Asian genealogical records and research in recent years is a particularly significant indication of that fact.

Genealogy in Asia

Under the leadership of Elder Theodore M. Burton, Assistant to the Council of the Twelve and vice-president and general manager of the Genealogical Society, a decision was reached in 1967 to establish Asian committees in the research department at the Society and later to place a full-time research specialist in charge of the Asian countries. This decision was prompted by a study conducted by Brigham Young University on the expected growth rate of the Church in the various countries of the world. The present growth rate in Asia is exceeding even those earlier expectations.

John W. Orton was chosen to head up the Asian area. His research, centered around Japanese emigrants, consisted of two weeks of study on the West Coast and in Hawaii. This trip also corresponded with the 1967 Japanese temple excursion.

During the latter part of October, 1967, Brother Orton visited depositories in the Midwest and East that are known to have large collections of Asian genealogical materials. It was

---

[12]Harrison T. Price, *Missionary Journal No. 3,* July 17, 1949, page 149.

also on this trip that he met Dr. Edward W. Wagner of Harvard University and Dr. William J. Schull of the University of Michigan, who offered ideas and suggestions for the study of Asian genealogical materials. The research department was made aware at that time of the principal American depositories of Asian materials: the University of Chicago Far Eastern Library, which houses a total of 7,000 volumes of Chinese local gazetteers, plus an impressive collection of Chinese biographies and genealogies; the Library of Congress, Orientalia Division, which has the largest collection of Chinese gazetteers in the United States, numbering a total of 3,500 titles, approximately 200 titles of clan genealogies, and printed biographies and other references for Japan and Korea; the East Asiatic Library of Columbia University, which houses the largest collection of Chinese clan genealogies in the world, according to Mr. T. K. Tong, head of the Chinese Section, and a collection of Chinese local gazetteers numbering 640 titles; and Harvard Yenching Library of Harvard University, which, chiefly because of Dr. Wagner, is actively collecting Korean genealogical materials and presently has civil service examination lists, early *Hi-juk* (census registers), and over 100 titles of Korean clan genealogies, as well as approximately 200 titles of Chinese clan genealogies and 3,000 titles of Chinese local gazetteers.

In the late spring of 1968, John Orton was accompanied by Tatsui Sato for five weeks of research and survey work in Japan, followed by two weeks of similar work in Korea. During the Japan portion of the trip they were extremely successful in getting information from government officers and record keepers, as well as private and public depositories in the Tokyo and Kyoto-Nara areas of Japan. The two weeks in Korea were added at the last minute, as it was felt that Brother Orton should take advantage of President Spencer Palmer's knowledge of Korean affairs. The time in Korea proved very useful in helping the Society become acquainted in that country as well as learn something of the unusually rich store of records and depositories there.

It was found that Korean family association headquarters

or libraries maintain current editions of clan genealogies. A small collection of approximately 1,000 volumes of *Chok-po* (clan genealogies) was located in a library inside the grounds of the Chang Kyung Palace. It was determined that to be effective it will be necessary that each title be catalogued and classified in such a manner that if duplicates are found in other depositories, they can be recognized.

In response to a suggestion initiated by Dr. Palmer, the Society has entered into a cooperative venture with Professor Edward Wagner of Harvard to microfilm the impressive collection of *Chok-po* on file in the Korean Central National Library in Seoul. Application has been made to the Ministry of Education of Korea. They have agreed and from that point on the project has been in the hands of Van A. Neiswender, the Genealogical Society's manager of the microfilm division, who is the officer of the records selection committee responsible for negotiating and signing filming contracts.

In the early spring of 1969, the research department undertook a brief survey of genealogical materials on deposit in the Philippines and made contacts with prospective participants in the World Conference on Records in Salt Lake City August 5 through 8, 1969, from the Philippines, Japan, Korea, Hong Kong, and Taiwan. In the Philippines the usual sources of civil registration, census, land records, tombstone inscriptions, etc., were explored, but there were two highlights on the trip: discovering that the Philippines is one of the few countries in Asia (perhaps the only one at present) that has an established functioning National Archives, and that there are still members living in some of the tribes in the mountain province that are able to recite their memorized genealogies. With the beginning of the fiscal year 1969 a small amount of money was approved for evaluating and determining the depository of important Korean clan genealogies.

Although the Japanese people have now completed several successful temple excursions to the Hawaii Temple, they have not had an instruction manual adapted to their customs and in their native language to assist them in completing their family group sheets. Lacking such a manual, local Saints took it upon themselves to write and publish one in Japanese. However, it was not adequate, so permission was granted for the research and the records adjustment departments of the Genealogical Society, which handle the processing of Japanese family group sheets, to jointly undertake the writing of such a manual. This manual will be written and a few copies published in English, then translated into Japanese for the use of the Saints in Japan.

Tatsui Sato now works full-time in the research department of the Society in Salt Lake City. He has been occupied with a Japanese surname catalog project and a Japanese royalty project. In compiling the pedigrees and family group sheets of royalty, it has been found that there are special problems involved and special sources to be consulted that are not known to the average researcher. As many genealogists are eventually able to trace at least one of their lines into royalty, and as family group sheets are submitted on these families from different patrons, the problems are multiplied. The Genealogical Society has established the policy that any royal lines that include the Imperial Family in Japan will be researched and submitted for processing by the staff of the Genealogical Society. Brother Sato's responsibility on this project is to compile from every source available the pedigree and family group sheets for the Imperial Family.

At present, Brother Sato is compiling the pedigree from printed sources. One problem he has encountered is that as he approaches the early Medieval Period, some of the sources disagree as to dates of birth and death. This is where original research will be required.

The Japanese surname catalog has developed into a complex project. For nearly three years, Brother Sato has been compiling surnames from various sources. The catalog now boasts a total of some 80,000 surnames. He is now arranging them in a useable form, with volume one completed and a projected total of ten to twelve volumes. The main purpose in the Genealogical Society's undertaking this project is to assist in clearing the names for temple work when Japan is included in the computerized GIANT program. It is also anticipated that the surname catalog will serve as a guide for Japanese and Westerners alike in correcting pronunciation and spelling.

Computers in Japan are now using Katakana characters, and the surnames will be written in both Kanji and Katakana characters in the surname catalog. The Hepburn method of Romanization has been adopted because this method is the easiest for the Westerner to use with the correct pronunciation. The completed catalog will contain the surname in Kanji, an alphabetical index in Romaji, and also an index by Stroke.

The Genealogical Society is now beginning to collect genealogical materials from Asia as they become available and known. The principal focus thus far has been upon Japan, because it is a modern country and convenient to visit, and because the Japanese Church members are engrossed in genealogy and have had greater exposure to English and the Church in America than have the Church members of other Asian countries.

But Chinese, Korean, and other peoples of Asia are not being ignored. Most of the Chinese clan genealogies that become available are being purchased. Professor Gary Williams of Brigham Young University is assisting in the evaluation of and the purchase of local Chinese gazetteers. In preparation for future acquisitions, the Society has also recently hired a Taiwan-Chinese member of the Church, a man who has his master's degree in library science, to work in cataloguing.

V

KOREA

KOREA

Never before in the history of the Church has there been such an unusual record of achievement as in Korea. Yet that country is farther removed and generally less well-known to the membership of the Church than any of its Asian neighbors. A mountainous peninsula about 600 miles long and 135 miles wide, Korea is located in northeastern Asia. Japan lies about 120 miles to the east. To the west across the Yellow Sea lies the coast of China. Seoul, the capital city of South Korea and location of the Korean Mission headquarters, is less than 30 miles from the demilitarized zone separating Communist North Korea from South Korea. The city, which is inland on the Han River, is growing rapidly and now has a population of about four million.

Of the 30 million people in the Republic of Korea, well over one and one-half million are Christians, the largest proportion in any Far Eastern country except the Philippines. About 500,000 of these are Catholics and 1,300,000 are Protestants. Initial reaction to Christianity in Korea, as in Japan, was hostile. The religion was actively persecuted by Yi Dynasty government from its introduction in the sixteenth century until after the signing of the Treaty of Friendship and Trade with the United States in 1884. Since that time, Christian missionary effort has made impressive contributions in the fields of education, medicine, and public welfare.

Korea has been one of the most productive mission fields of The Church of Jesus Christ of Latter-day Saints, although compared with Japan and China, it is a very new field of labor. The first Mormon missionaries arrived in Seoul in April, 1956; the mission was established in July, 1962.

Today the Korean Mission comprises more than 4,000 first-generation Latter-day Saints situated in twenty congregations throughout South Korea. These Korean members are unusual in many ways. Racially they are one of the most homogeneous people in the world. And a more highly educated membership can be found in few other places in the Church. The Korean people's thirst for knowledge and their study of the scriptures are proverbial and come from a long and rich tradition.[1] Elder Spencer W. Kimball of the Council of the Twelve, among others of the General Authorities, gave notice of this fact in his personal diary after a visit to Seoul on February 27, 1968:

> We find the Koreans are ravenous in their appetite for knowledge and many of them have degrees and some of them doctor's degrees. They are a well groomed and attractive people.

Following an official tour of the missions of the Church in Asia in 1969, Elder Ezra Taft Benson made a similiar observation:

> The missions of Asia are getting high-type, devoted converts. One little branch of 50 members in Kwangju, Korea, has five college professors.

The Korean Mission is unusual in other ways as well. It is perhaps still the only mission of the Church where more men than women have been baptized, and where there has been an especially strong potential for priesthood leadership and growth by reason of convert baptisms.

It is a paradox that the Church in Korea had its beginnings because of war and the influx of Latter-day Saint "combat missionaries." These were young men deeply dedicated to their country and to God. Some were returned missionaries and others looked upon their Korea tour of duty as an opportunity to serve the purposes of their Heavenly Father. They met with wonderful success among the Koreans because they generated love and their faith showed forth

---

[1]Edwin O. Reischauer and John K. Fairbank, *East Asia: The Great Tradition* (Boston: Houghton Mifflin Co., 1960), p. 343, conclude: ". . . the literary bias of Chinese civilization resulted in a greater emphasis on formal education in East Asia than in other major zones of civilization. Within East Asia, however, the Koreans seem to have emphasized formal education even more than the Chinese."

clearly in their conduct; the people were ready to receive their messages of encouragement.

The Lord has declared that "all things must come to pass in their time" (D&C 64:32), and in Korea the 1950s and 1960s were a favorable time. The Latter-day Saint GI's brought compassion and brotherhood to a people who were completely torn by the agonies of a fratricidal war. More than 300,000 Korean soldiers had lost their lives in the struggle, two million civilians had been killed, wounded, or were missing, and hundreds of thousands were barely existing in pathetic refugee camps on the outskirts of the big cities. The GI brethren wanted to help. On their own volition they sought to share the light of the gospel with the Korean people. They gave their money and their time.

Between 1951 and 1955 these servicemen attained success without the aid of any full-time missionaries or the benefit of Church literature of any kind in the native language. They opened the way and, under the inspiration of the Lord, laid the foundation for the establishment of the Korean Mission. The initial labor was centered at Pusan, the largest port city in Korea, on the southern tip of the peninsula. In those years it was a gathering place for displaced persons seeking escape from the ravages of war in the north. It was here that in January, 1952, the servicemen offered English language and gospel investigator classes. These were advertised in the local schools, and by the end of that year attendance reached a peak of 327 Korean students and 32 GI's during one evening alone.

The first results were realized on August 3, 1952, when four Koreans were baptized at Songdo near Pusan. Two of these were a son and daughter of Dr. Kim Ho Jik, [2] the first Korean convert to the Church, who had been baptized in the United States earlier. Dr. Kim's inspirational story is told later.

During the month of September, as a result of the cease-fire agreement, Seoul National University was returned to Seoul from Pusan, where it had taken temporary refuge.

---

[2]In accordance with customary practice, Korean surnames will appear before given names in this book.

It was discovered that almost all of the new members and their friends were actually natives of Seoul, and with the return of the university there, only one member out of a total of 27 declared his intention of remaining in Pusan.

During 1953-1955 proselyting continued at a vigorous rate. In November, 1953, a devasting fire destroyed one-fourth of downtown Pusan, leaving over 40,000 Koreans homeless. This disaster sparked new missionary efforts, including study classes and monthly socials to which Koreans were invited. In late 1954 and early 1955 there was impressive growth in new memberships. Some of those baptized have remained faithful in the Church over the years. Among them are Park Jae Am, Oh Ke Hi, Choi Jae Sin, Kook Yung Gill, and Kim Do Pil.

Kim Ho Jik

Dr. Kim Ho Jik, the first Korean to be baptized into the Church, is probably the most distinguished and influential leader of Oriental ancestry thus far converted in East Asia. More than any other single man he was the father and prime moving force in the establishment of the Korean Mission.

Elder Gordon B. Hinckley has observed that Brother Kim's name "will always occupy a place of prominence in the annals of the Church in the Orient."[3] President Paul C. Andrus reported from Tokyo in September, 1956: "Brother Ho Jik Kim is very influential and plays a vital role in getting the Church established in Korea."

With Dr. Kim's sudden passing on August 31, 1959, one of his many student converts paid him this simple tribute: "His righteous influence and simple faith in God was a great light for the people of Korea.[4] These words of Young B. Lee, who was then at Brigham Young University, reflect the high esteem in which Brother Kim was held by a newly risen generation of Korean Saints, at that time primarily students, as well as by his fellow countrymen with whom he associated in high political and social office, and by a host of Latter-day Saint servicemen who came under his influence in Korea.

---

[3]*The Improvement Era,* March 1964, p. 181.
[4]*Church News,* September 12, 1959.

Dr. Kim's conversion story attests to the mysterious workings of the Spirit of the Lord among the faithful in Asia. His considerable talents and his dedicated contributions to the Church are without counterpart elsewhere in the Asian missions of the Church.

He was born into a Confuciañ home in north Pyong-an Province on April 16, 1905. From early boyhood he eagerly sought the truth. His search first led him to Ch'ondogyo, a native eclectic faith much in vogue at the time, and later to Buddhism. These failed to satisfy him. In 1925 he joined the Presbyterian church and served as an elder for a period of time. Here again his spiritual needs were unfulfilled. Thus, according to one report,[5] he resolved to journey to America with a dual purpose in mind: to seek out the "real religion"— the one that would satisfy his conscience—and to gain further knowledge in nutritional science.

Kim Ho Jik had received his undergraduate education at the Suwon Agricultural and Forestry College and at the Tohoku Imperial University in Korea before going to the USA. Between 1950 and 1951 he attended Cornell University at Ithaca, New York, where he received his M.A. and Ph.D. degrees. It was during this time that a member of the Church, Oliver Wayman, reached out in friendship to this Korean student and invited him to attend Latter-day Saint meetings. One day Brother Kim asked Brother Wayman if he had any literature that would tell him about the tenets of his faith.

To quote from Brother Wayman's recollection of that incident:

> Knowing that he was a devout and studious Presbyterian, I gave him a copy of Dr. James E. Talmage's *Articles of Faith*. Within a week he had read the book and asked for more. He told me it was the best book on the gospel he had ever read and that he believed it thoroughly. I gave him a copy of the Book of Mormon, which he read in a very short time. He accepted it as the word of God along with the Bible, but said the Book of Mormon was much easier to understand and more complete. Clyde Richards and I encouraged him to attend our services and he agreed. However, we found that our services were just

---

[5]See Paul H. Maxwell, "Suffer It to Be So Now," *Improvement Era*, March 1954, pp. 151ff.

a short time earlier than the Presbyterian services. So, he would come to our sacrament meeting and leave during the latter part of the opening exercises to attend his own church. This continued until I left.

On the day I was leaving Cornell, I met him in the corridor as Clyde and I were talking. I felt impelled to ask Dr. Kim if he knew why he had left his home, family and a good position in Korea to come to the U.S. . . . .

His answer was that he supposed that it was to get the newer knowledge of agriculture that his country needed so much and help disseminate it to his people.

I then bore my testimony of the gospel and told him that it was my opinion that *the Lord had moved upon him to come to America at the opportunity presented to him in order that he might receive the gospel and take it back to his people in preparation for a great missionary work to be done there.* He had received the gospel but had been unwilling to accept it through repentance and baptism but wanted to carry the truths he had learned to the Presbyterian church for its reform. This I informed him would not work and that if he refused to do the work the Lord had for him to do, another would be raised up in his place. *I have seldom felt the Spirit as strongly as I did at that time and knew that what I was telling him was true.* That was the last time we saw each other. (Italics are author's.)

Dr. Kim read the Book of Mormon again, and the Spirit bore witness to him of its truth. He was baptized in the Susquehanna River near the place where Joseph Smith and Oliver Cowdery had been baptized. As Brother Kim came up out of the water, he reported that the inspired testimony of Brother Wayman was substantiated by a voice saying to him, "Feed my sheep, feed my sheep."

On the flyleaf of his triple combination, under the record of his baptism, he later wrote the notation: "Words Given—Feed my Sheep."

He was ordained a deacon on August 5, 1951, and a priest on August 26, 1951. In September, 1951, he returned home.

When Dr. Kim returned to Korea he was immediately given high responsibility in education and government, including the positions of president of the National Fisheries College in Pusan; vice-minister of education in Syngman Rhee's cabinet; chief Korean delegate to UNESCO, where he represented Korea in India and other foreign assignments; professor at various universities; and dean and president of several colleges. He also served as dean of the College of Animal Husbandry at Konguk University and president of the Seoul City Board of Education. He was author of six highly regarded publications. The latest at Cornell University, in March, 1951, was entitled *Device of High Protein: A Low-cost Diet for Orientals.*

Dr. Kim has repeated the following incident:

One Sunday while he (Dr. Kim) was vice-minister of education, Korean President Syngman Rhee sent his secretary in the President's personal car to find Brother Kim and bring him to the presidential palace to discuss an important matter that had arisen. The secretary found Brother Kim teaching a Mormon Sunday School class. Brother Kim told him he would have to wait until church was over before he could accompany him. When Brother Kim finally met President Rhee, he was chastized for causing such a delay. Brother Kim explained to him and the others assembled that because of the importance of his assignment as a Sunday School teacher, he had to finish his lesson before he could answer the summons. Whereupon President Rhee patted him on the shoulder and said, *"Chalhaeso!"* (You did well.)

Brother Kim was a widely acclaimed authority on nutrition and particularly the nutritional value of the soybean. As a result of this, he was asked to represent Korea at an international FAO meeting in India in August, 1959. He took advantage of the plane trip and some of his leisure time there to carry out part of his New Year's resolution to reread the Book of Mormon. Mosiah, Chapter 20 was marked with the date August 8, 1959.

Upon Dr. Kim's arrival home from India, Brother Rhee Ho Nam, who later became first counselor in the Korean Mission presidency, remarked to him that he looked very tired. Brother Kim answered that he had not felt well in India and that he had been anxious to get home because he did not want to die in India. Brother Grant Heaton, who was then president of the Southern Far East Mission, substantiates Brother Kim's premonition. He stated that at the time of Brother Kim's visit on his way home, Brother Kim was very restless. In answer to President Heaton's query, Brother Kim had told him that it was important that he get home as soon as possible.

Less than a month later Brother Kim was dead. He passed away suddenly on August 31, 1959.

Having heard the voice speak the words that had been uttered to other disciples long ago, "Feed my sheep," Brother Kim had lived long enough to be a major tool in bringing the gospel to Korea and aiding the Church in gaining a foothold there. He was an inspiration to a predominantly young membership. There are many who still cherish his counsel to them and experiences of association with him in humble places where many of lesser fame would not have gone. Brother Kim associated with these young people on their level and in so doing taught them great lessons in humility, devotion, and faithfulness. There is a verse shaded in red in Brother Kim's copy of the Doctrine and Covenants bearing a date less than a month before he died. Its message is made even more significant by his life. It reads: "Every man, seeking the interest of his neighbor, and doing all things with an eye single to the glory of God."

A worthy conclusion to Brother Kim's story is this sincere tribute and testimony:

A TRIBUTE

To LDS servicemen who have served in Korea

Every Korean person looks upon you with their joyful eyes, even with tears of gratitude. What a wonderful work you have done in the past and are now doing. The Korean saints have all been converted directly or indirectly through your honest efforts and sincere conduct. They followed your directions that they might become more like you in their lives sooner or later if they are sincere enough. You LDS servicemen opened a wonderful chance to serve the people and promote your faith. Whatever may be the task, the results are good for you and for the Korean people.

On August 2, 1955, the land of Korea was dedicated for the preaching of the gospel, culminating several years of effort and teaching by the servicemen. On this wonderful occasion I remembered many fine brothers and sisters who had been working for years for the salvation of Korean souls throughout Korea, in Seoul, at Pusan and other places. There are many unforgettable figures who have returned to the States already: Brother Erickson,

Brother Bradshaw, Chaplain Covington, who were pioneers at the very beginning with the Korean group at Pusan; then Brother Gibbons, Chaplains Madsen and Palmer and Brother Beck and Brother Fisher at the Seoul Group. Wherever they may be, their sweet thoughtfulness always makes us happy. The spirit of their love always preaches us the wonderful gospel and encourages and comforts us.

I firmly believe that the LDS Church is the true Church on the earth and was restored by Joseph Smith, Jr., the Prophet of God. The Book of Mormon is the word of God, and it was correctly translated by Joseph Smith. God exists and reveals to us what we ought to do at this time, if we ask him sincerely.

I do this in the name of our Lord, Jesus Christ. Amen.

> Elder Ho Jik Kim
> President of the Korean District
> 1955

Elder Lee's Significant Visit

Elder Harold B. Lee of the Council of the Twelve made a memorable week-long visit to Korea during the first part of September, 1954, and under appointment of the First Presidency investigated the advisability of opening Korea as an independent, full-time mission. He was impressed with the work of the LDS chaplains and servicemen and with the testimonies of the new Korean members of the Church.

Elder Harold B. Lee in Korea, September, 1954, with Hilton A. Robertson, Kim Ho Jik, and five LDS chaplains. Front, Grant Mann, Robertson, Lee, and Kim; back, Richard H. Henstrom, Spencer J. Palmer, John R. Connell, and Mark L. Money.

In this October general conference report in the Salt Lake Tabernacle, Elder Lee noted that sufficient funds had been raised each month by servicemen in the Far East to sustain 21 full-time missionaries in the Japanese mission. As the direct result of the work of these brethren, 47 converts were baptized in that mission during 1953 alone. Elder Lee referred repeatedly to the "miraculous power of divine intervention that is out there" in Asia. His two-month Oriental tour had taken him 21,000 miles, including a demanding schedule of meetings in various battlefield regions of Korea. In reviewing this challenging and revealing experience, Brother Lee offered this significant witness: "The signs of divinity are in the Far East. The work of the Almighty is increasing with a tremendous surge."[6] And such proved to be the case in Korea. His report set the stage for the dedication of that land for missionary work.

The Dedication

Standing on a high hill overlooking a shrine dedicated to servicemen who gave their lives in defense of their homeland, President Joseph Fielding Smith of the Council of the Twelve officially dedicated Korea for the preaching of the gospel on Tuesday, August 2, 1955.

According to Rodney W. Fye, who was present, this prayer was filled with great power. President Smith literally commanded Satan to free the land from his chains that it might become choice through the preaching of the gospel of Jesus Christ. He prayed particularly for a blessing upon the Korean membership, which up to that time had been under the charge of the servicemen's organization, that they would prepare themselves to accept responsibility for the opening of the nation to a reception of truth. All present were made keenly aware of the political, economic, and social convulsions that had gripped Korea in recent history. President Smith promised that stability would return again. There was a sense of relief among those present that the gospel would at last be planted in that country,

---

[6]See Harold B. Lee, "Miraculous Power of Divine Intervention Present in Orient," *Church News*, October 9, 1954, p. 8: also Chaplains Spencer J. Palmer and John R. Connell, Jr., "Elder Lee Visits Korea," *Church News*, October 2, 1954, pp.7ff.

since many had wondered in times past if this blessing could ever be realized. Those present were deeply impressed with the harsh beauty of the setting as they stood in a rather relaxed circle and felt the Spirit of the Lord upon that occasion.

To begin full-time missionary work in Korea, it was determined that American elders laboring in Japan should be sent there. However, Korean visas were not easily secured. One could not qualify without a guarantee of support from an established organization, and the Church had no Korean organization. Dr. Kim helpfully intervened, the first of many such services rendered by him on behalf of the Church in dealing with the government. The officials accepted his personal guarantee, and in April, 1956, visas were granted for Elders Richard L. Detton and Don G. Powell, the first to labor in the Korean District of the newly organized Northern Far East Mission. Upon their arrival, these brethren were met by Dr. Kim, who had been set apart as president of the Korean Dis-

Joseph Fielding Smith dedicates Korea for the opening of full-time missionary work, August 2, 1955. Pictured here on a hill overlooking Korea's war-torn capital city of Seoul are, left to right, front row, Rodney W. Fye, servicemen's supervisor in Korea; Chris E. Case; Kim Ho Jik, president of tne newly formed Korea District; Elder Smith; Lt. Col. Robert H. Slover, LDS Far East servicemen's supervisor, who was appointed Korean Mission president in 1968; President Hilton A. Robertson of the Northern Far East Mission; and back row, Brother Soker Lee, Captain Vernon J. Tipton, and H. Grant Heaton, en route to his assignment as the first president of the newly created Southern Far East Mission.

trict, and by about thirty other members of the Church who had been praying for the missionaries' coming. At that time there were 64 members of record, located principally in Seoul and Pusan, where branches were organized during President Smith's visit. Six other elders entered during the summer months, including Elder Gail E. Carr, who later became the first president of the Korean Mission.

These pioneer missionaries labored under harsh conditions. They faced many disadvantages and inconveniences. In the first place, the Korean language was completely new to all of them. In addition, they had to rely on English tracts or Japanese translations in a country where English was not generally understood and where Japanese suffered the opprobium of being the language of the former conquerors. There were no available Korean language texts, no missionary lesson materials. When a new elder arrived, he simply had to rely on the Lord and the competency of his senior companion to teach him everything. Dr. Kim's translations of the thirteen Articles of Faith and the sacrament prayers during those initial years are still in use in Korea today.

Living conditions were poor. Housing was at a premium, and obtaining healthful food was a great problem. But the missionaries' faith was firmly anchored in a conviction that God had revealed to them that their work in Korea was great in his sight.

F. Ray Hawkins, one of these first missionaries, recounts a poignant example of their devotion to the gospel cause among the Korean people. In the summer of 1958, when half of the ten missionaries in Korea had been striken with hepatitis, President Paul C. Andrus came from Tokyo to meet with the missionaries. After expressing his own concern and that of the General Authorities and of parents and relatives for their health and well being, he asked each elder to express himself concerning whether or not to close the Korean District of the Northern Far East Mission. Each missionary in turn arose and in a most inspiring spirit expressed his willingness to give his life, if necessary, for the furtherance of the work in Korea. Section 103 of the Doctrine and Covenants, verses 27 and 28, were invoked: "Let no man be afraid to lay down his life for my sake; for whoso layeth down his life for my sake shall find it again. And whoso is not willing to lay down his life for my sake is not my disciple." Each of those present reported feeling the Spirit of the Lord in rich abundance, testifying that he had a work for them to perform in the Land of the Morning Calm.

Between the establishment of the Korean District of the Northern Far East Mission in 1955 and the beginning of the Korean Mission in 1962, there were five district presidents: Kim Ho Jik, from 1955 until his death in late 1959; Elder Lowell E. Brown, 1960-61, during which time he also served as second counselor in the mission presidency; James E. Bradshaw, 1961-62; Lynn Waddell, from 1962 until the arrival of Gail E. Carr.

Earliest Korea missionaries: back row, right to left: Gail E. Carr, who later became the first Korean Mission president; Don G. Powell; Paul C. Andrus, president of the Northern Far East Mission, of which Korea was a district at the time of this picture; Richard Detton; Larry D. Orme. Front row: Newel E. Kimball, Claude W. Newman, Karl C. Fletcher, and Dean M. Anderson.

Gail Carr's historic contributions to the development of the Church in Korea have been succinctly expressed by Elder Gordon B. Hinckley:

> Brother Carr first was called to work in Japan and then was sent to Korea, where he was one of that early group who opened

the work when Dr. Kim returned to Korea. The missionaries lived under the most adverse and difficult circumstances, but through all of this adversity there developed an undying love for these tremendous people who had suffered so much.

When the decision was made to establish Korea as a separate mission, Gail E. Carr was called to preside and his young wife was called to accompany him. Sister Hinckley and I were with them during those early days of their mission. When their child arrived, they were living under difficult circumstances, but there was never a complaint. He was instrumental in securing the present location of the mission headquarters, a beautiful property with spacious grounds within ten minutes of the heart of the great city of Seoul. I have never seen a time when Gail Carr was not bubbling with enthusiasm concerning the saints, the missionaries, and the opportunities in Korea.

When Spencer J. Palmer arrived in Korea to undertake the leadership of the Korean Mission on August 2, 1965, he was returning to a land where he had served the Church as an Army chaplain ten years earlier, and a country where he was well acquainted with members and Church beginnings. And, as a Brigham Young University professor specializing in Korean studies and Oriental religions, he was known by name in Korean academic and governmental circles.

Conditions in the Church in Korea in 1965 were much improved over the dismal war years, thanks to the leadership of President Carr between 1962 and 1965. The Church by this time owned land and buildings, including a beautiful and well-situated mission headquarters in Seoul. Missionary work had been opened in Taegu and greatly expanded in Seoul and Pusan. Through the combined efforts of President Carr and construction supervisors Rex A. Cheney (Far East area supervisor) and Kenneth Roos (Korean area supervisor), work was well underway toward the completion of the first Mormon chapel in Korea, at Seoul East Branch.

But there were problems, too. Church membership consisted primarily of young students. Thus the mission was vibrant, but the membership was relatively unstable. Mutual Improvement Association activities were well attended, but the young branches suffered from lack of Korean leadership and thus were entirely dependent upon the young American

Seoul East Chapel in Korea, the first Latter-day Saint Chapel on the Asian continent, dedicated by Elder Gordon B. Hinckley of the Council of the Twelve, September 10, 1966.

elders. Another difficulty was the lack of available restoration scriptures in the Korean language. Because English was commonly taught, the missionaries used it as a proselyting tool. Mormon family life was practically nonexistent, though much groundwork had been laid. The mission existed primarily apart from native Korean society.

A number of ambitious goals were pursued in the Korean Mission between 1965 and 1968: to naturalize the Church in Korea, to improve its image and influence among leaders of Korean society, to develop stability in the branches and districts through greater Korean participation in mission affairs, to increase the membership, to extend the proselyting field into the outlying provinces of the country, and to make provision for the translation and publication of the scriptures of the restored Church into the Korean language.

The Use of Mass Media

Preparations began in the early fall of 1965 to take advantage of the mass media—radio, television, and newspapers—for publicizing the Church and spreading its message to the Korean public.

I. Music and Christmas Programs

In December, 1965, all Korea missionaries were invited to the mission home for a special three-day Christmas reunion and to examine various phases of missionary work. After enjoying a contata prepared by the Korean District MIA, the elders visited the U.S. Eighth Army Hospital to sing Christmas carols as a gesture of appreciation for past services performed for the missionaries there. This experience led to singing visits to the homes of several Korean members, culminating in a special presentation of songs beside the large City Hall Plaza Christmas tree. The Korean response was very warm for such a bitter-cold evening. Thus a Korean Mission tradition was born in which the elders literally took "to the air" each year to present the spirit of Christmas to the people of Korea.

On January 2, 1966, President Palmer and District President Rhee, along with a newly formed Korean District Choir, presented a half-hour program over KBS-TV called "The Mormon Church in Korea." Television instruments were set up in various convenient locations in the Seoul area, including Chung Woon and Tong Bu chapels, so that all members of the Church were able to watch. The choir's opening hymn (in Korean) was "Come, Come Ye Saints," after which President Palmer responded to five questions posed by Brother Rhee: 1) Are Mormons Christians? 2) Do Mormons believe in the Christian Trinity? 3) What do Mormons believe about the Bible? 4) What is the Book of Mormon? 5) What about temple work for the living and the dead?

The members were particularly inspired and considered it a highlight of this national TV program to see a picture of the Prophet Joseph Smith on their screens as the choir sang "Praise to the Man" in the background. The program closed with President Palmer's bearing testimony to the truthfulness of the restored Church and inviting the Korean citizenry to learn more about its message through the missionaries.

This program was only the beginning. Largely through the efforts of Elders Alan G. Perriton of New Zealand and Steven R. Robinson of Elko, Nevada, and drawing heavily upon the musical talents of Chong T'ae Pan as chorus director, the Korean Church membership and the missionaries presented many Christmas programs over radio and television. These included Tong Yang (TBC), Mun Hwa (MBC), and Chung Ang (KBS), plus the American Forces Korea Network TV. No other group in Korea received so much coverage and so much favorable notice in the news in connection with the Christmas seasons. The Tong Yang radio program was rebroadcast among the forces of the Republic of Korea in Vietnam.

Major public performances of the singing Mormon missionaries in December, 1967, included the International Friendship Association, the United States Information Service Christmas program, two telecasts, and three radio programs. The singing elders also joined the U.S. Army Band and the Seoul Metropolitan Children's Choir in a mammoth three-and-a-half-hour program in Seoul's principal auditorium, Citizen's Hall. Elder Marion D. Hanks' fervent witness of Christ to the Korean people was an especially appreciated feature of one of the programs of that year. That was also the year that missionary caroling in downtown Seoul received excellent notice in Korean newspapers. One of the participating missionaries, Elder Mark A. Peterson, wrote of this experience in the mission publication.

> This year's escapade had to be the best in history because of the excitement it caused among the throngs that gathered around wherever the group stopped to wassail. A reporter from the Dong-A Ilbo newspaper was snooping around town looking for the news that might break through the night at any moment.
>
> There was an air of expectancy as myriads mingled shoulder to shoulder amidst the bright neon lights of Myong Dong, a popular area in downtown Seoul. Suddenly from out of the east and down the hill came an army of 64 missionaries roughly grouped in one column, four abreast, singing at the top of their voices. The masses formed a path for the elders as they took up their positions to sing and a crowd quickly gathered.

Some were taking pictures of us. The reporter approached the most obvious person on the fringe of the group and it happened to be me. He asked in apprehensive Korean, "What are you doing?"

The depth of the question caught me off guard, but after taking a moment to think I resumed my natural cool and answered, "We're singing."

The reporter ventured further, "Yes, but why? What is the objective?

His questions were embarrassing me and besides I wanted to get back to singing instead of talking.

"The reason? It's Christmas."

The reporter seemed to be taken back by my razor-sharp logic, but he asked me one last question, "Do you do like this in America?"

After the reporter received the "of course" answer, he walked away, busily scribbling notes.

The next day newspapers announced that Mormon missionaries love to sing and are highly motivated in their faith. The Koreans, often called "The Welsh of Asia" because of their fondness for music, were highly pleased.

II. Music and the Spoken Word

Since May, 1968, the Mormon Tabernacle Choir program has been broadcast over Korean radio each Saturday afternoon, with the messages of Richard L. Evans delivered in the Korean language. No doubt this is the only foreign language mission of Asia, and perhaps of the world, in which this program reaches the native public on a weekly basis. Lee Kui Ja of KBS radio produces the program.

This opportunity was arranged through the son of one of the early Pusan converts, Sister Kim Do Pil, whose son, Lee Sang Pack, a non-Mormon, is on the staff of KBS radio. Working through Murray Hoki, Asia coordinator of Bonneville International in Salt Lake City, Elder Steven Robinson received weekly copies of the Choir broadcast script. These were translated by Brother Ji Yong Dal of the mission office staff in Seoul, who also prepared the spoken word portion of the program the first year.

New Areas and New Leaders

In 1965 the Korean Mission consisted of one district comprising seven branches. Four branches were in the capital, three of which were located close to the mission home: Sam Chung, Chung Woon, Seoul West, and Seoul East. One branch was in Taegu and two were in Pusan: Pusan and Pusan Tong Ku. At the conclusion of President Palmer's time in Korea in 1968, the mission had been divided into two districts, comprising a combined total of 13 branches and three dependent groups.

The Southern District with headquarters in Pusan was organized in February, 1968, with Bae Young Chon as president; Elder David Ashworth, first counselor; Do Gil Hwe, second counselor, and Elder So Won, secretary. This widely scattered district included four branches—Pusan, Pusan Tong Ku, Taegu, Kwangju—and two areas, Tong Nae and Chon Ju.

The Central District, with headquarters in Seoul, embraced eight branches: Sam Chung, Chung Woon, Seoul West, Seoul East, Seoul East Gate, Nok Bon, Young Dung Po, Taejon, and two areas, Shin Chon and Inchon. The presidency of this newly formed district comprised Dr. Cha Jong Hwan, president; Park Jae Am, first counselor; Lee Jae Soo, second counselor; and Hwang Jong Sup, secretary.

In line with mission policy for the missionaries to seek out heads of families, older investigators, and friends for the Church, the average age level of new converts to the Church rose gradually by five years during the three-year period of President Palmer's service. Families began coming into the Church. Among these were some men of position. Consequently, branch presidencies and high councils could be staffed with capable priesthood holders. The payment of tithes between 1965 and 1967 increased by 305%. Membership increased from 2,529 in 1965 to 3,317 in 1968, a 31% increase. Significant changes in membership began to be apparent. Elder Gordon B. Hinckley, who had been associated with Korea Church developments from the beginnings of the mission, made note of this in October, 1966, at the dedication of Seoul East Branch. In a letter to the First Presidency, he wrote:

This is the first building ever built by the Church on the continent of Asia. It was filled to capacity with some five hundred in attendance, including a number of prominent men—the editor of the *Korea Times*, clergymen of other churches, community leaders. The building was constructed under the labor missionary program. By Korean standards it is an excellent building.

But the most inspiring thing was the congregation. For the first time I felt that we are making some real headway here. We now have some men and women of genuine ability who are members of the Church and who are becoming leaders in the Church here. The mission president's counselors are local men, the district presidency are local men, and all seven branches are presided over by local men. The new building is a credit to the Church, but the membership is a greater credit.

President Brown's Historic Visit

The Korea phase of President Hugh B. Brown's historic tour of the Asian missions in 1966 began on April 26. Sixty-two missionaries were on hand to greet him at Kimpo airport, as well as scores of Saints, servicemen, and members of the public press. Throughout the tour President Brown was a man with a mission and a message. In the afternoon of the first day he addressed the United Graduate School of Theology at Yonsei University, an institution of higher learning established many years before by Protestant missionaries. The initial reception was understandably reserved, for this was the first time a Mormon elder had been invited to speak. But barriers were quickly dispelled by President Brown's engaging spirit and masterful eloquence:

We believe that men are the children of God in a real sense, and that does not apply to any group coming from any particular country. We believe that all men are children of God and therefore are or should be brothers. In fact, it is quite common in the Church to refer to one another as "brother" or "sister," based on the idea that with a common God we are brothers and sisters. . . .

We think, as a people, that the Reformation was not comparable to, nor did it constitute a restoration. A restoration of the gospel was necessitated by the withdrawal of the gospel. And a restoration of the gospel came about in later days. That is our message—that in our time there came a great visitation from the heavens in which God the Father and the Son appeared and spoke to man. As a result of that great vision, other heavenly beings

President Hugh B. Brown, of the First Presidency, with Elder Gordon B. Hinckley, supervisor of Oriental missions, and Korean Mission President Spencer J. Palmer, at Kimpo International Airport, April 26, 1966.

came, and there was organized what is called the Mormon Church. Now it may sound a bit presumptous of us to intimate that the Mormon Church is the true church, but I just remind you that either a church, any church, is true or it is false.

That same evening President Brown and Elder Hinckley arrived at Seoul East Chapel, where they were greeted by an excited, overflowing crowd of investigators, servicemen, members, and missionaries. As he rose to speak, the power of love radiated from President Brown's person to all those assembled. They felt the mantle of his authority through the power of this message:

> I come to you from President David O. McKay. He could not come personally so he asked me to come in his stead and represent him. . . .
> The Mormon people have been gathered together from all nations because of their faith in God and in the restoration of the gospel. I come to talk about a church that is universal. It is the Church of Jesus Christ for all the world, and he recognizes no distinction among the peoples of the world. He is no respecter of persons. . . .

> I ask the Lord to bless you people. Father in heaven, bless the people of Korea. They have come up through sorrow and disappointment and defeat, and yet they have come back and made good. Enable them to reap the blessings that come from the faithful observance of Thy laws.

Members had traveled from the most distant regions of South Korea to hear the venerable servant of the Lord. Their hearts were filled to overflowing, and his physical presence was undeniable evidence that the General Authorities at the hub in America really cared for them.

On Thursday, the last full day of his historic visit, President Brown met with the missionaries and also participated in a flag-raising ceremony. The vice-mayor of Seoul raised the Korean national flag over the headquarters property of the Church. Mr. Lee Kap Sung, only surviving member of the original signers of the famous 1919 Korean Declaration of Independence, spoke on the meaning of the national flag to citizens of the Republic of Korea. President Brown then challenged the Korean Saints to be patriotic citizens, to set an example by serving the Lord through serving the best interests of their country.

The Korean Mission Today

Robert H. Slover, third president of the Korean Mission, began his labors in early August of 1968. President Slover was a professor of political science at Brigham Young University at the time of his call; he had previously served as an army officer in Korea and received a commendation from the government for his work in the civil affairs/military government of the United States armed forces. He is a distinguished alumnus of Harvard University.

Under President Slover's leadership, the Korean Mission has experienced phenomenal growth. Baptisms during 1968-69 jumped to 450 and in 1969-70 climbed to 550. Average baptisms per year per missionary had reached 7.1 at the end of 1969. The missionary force has been considerably increased, reaching nearly one hundred. New proselyting areas have been opened. These have included Chinhae-Masan, Ch'un

Ch'on, and Kunsan, with others in prospect. New branches have been organized in Inch'on and Ch'onju. And there has been a strong and salutary emphasis upon teaching the Korean leadership the procedures of the Church.

Under the capable hands of Kenneth Roos and the Far Eastern construction supervisor, Marvin S. Harding, a new chapel at Pusan now not only serves the needs of local branch members but is also headquarters for the Southern District. This lovely building was dedicated in October, 1969, by President Bruce R. McConkie of the First Council of Seventy. Other new chapels are also being planned in the mission.

The impressive growth of the Church in Korea under Robert Slover's presidency is indicated in the announcement of establishment of a new, third district in the mission—the Honam District, with headquarters in Kwangju. Lee Jaesu was called as the first president of this district.

In times past Korea has been characterized as a sad and unpromising land. But since the dedication of that country for the preaching of the gospel by President Joseph Fielding Smith in 1955, conditions have greatly changed. A new nation has begun to rise. New vitality and hope have begun to take root among the Korean people, and for the first time in history there are encouraging prospects for the work of the Lord in the Land of the Morning Calm. In terms of baptisms per missionary, the Korean and Philippines missions are the fastest growing in Asia.

In 1966 President Hugh B. Brown delivered a sobering promise regarding the future of the Church in Korea, when he said:

> The time will come when tens of thousands of people will join the Church of Jesus Christ in this land and will receive the blessings of the gospel by living its principles.

Signs of fulfillment of that wonderful prophecy have already begun to appear.

VI

The PHILIPPINES

The PHILIPPINES

In 1965 a celebration was held in Cebu City commemorating the fourth century of the "Christianization of the Philippines." That same month marked the fourth anniversary of the opening of these islands to the missionaries of The Church of Jesus Christ of Latter-day Saints.

The Philippines is unique in Asia: It is the only Christian nation. More than 90% of the more than 35 million population are nominally Christian. The great majority are Roman Catholic, reflecting long years of Spanish rule. Furthermore, the Philippines is regarded as the third largest English-speaking country in the world, outranked only by the United States and England. The prevalence of the English language is evidence of the influence that the United States has had since the turn of the century, and particularly the years of American occupation after World War II.

The more than 7,000 islands constitute the Philippines in a land area one and one half times that of Utah. If the islands were superimposed over the Intermountain West, the islands would touch every state. Luzon is the largest of the nine major islands and is half the size of Utah in square miles.

Church history in the Philippine Islands began with the liberation of the country from the Japanese by the American landings on Leyte October 20, 1944, culminating in the fall of Manila in February, 1945. From the outset servicemen's group leaders organized LDS meetings, the first at Tacloban on the coast and at Samar, a U.S. Navy installation. These meetings were frequently interrupted by air raids and other exigencies of war. The first LDS conference was conducted by a Mormon chaplain with 50 in attendance. Some of the earliest meetings were held in the home of Peter and Maxine Grimm, long-time residents and staunch supporters of Church developments there.

Peter and Maxine Grimm, prominent in the development of the Church in the Philippines and Southeast Asia.

In October, 1951, Vinal G. Mauss, Japan Mission president, presided over a servicemen's conference with 45 in attendance. The Luzon Servicemen's District was officially organized on February 13, 1953, and conferences were held whenever possible. There were Church groups at Clark Air Force Base, Sangley Point, and Subic Bay. The Clark group was the largest and had functioning auxiliaries, including the first organized Relief Society in the Philippines.

In early June, 1954, the Luzon District was visited by the new Japan Mission president, Hilton A. Robertson, and his wife. In September of that year Elder Harold B. Lee visited, attended a special conference, and confirmed a newly baptized young Filipino mother into the Church.

President Joseph Fielding Smith, as part of his Asian tour, dedicated the Philippine Islands for the preaching of the gospel, at Clark Air Base on August 21, 1955. He was accompanied by his wife, Jessie Evans Smith, President and Sister Robertson, and H. Grant Heaton and his wife and child.

Six years after President Smith dedicated the islands for the preaching of the gospel, the tedious work of legally registering the Church in the Philippines was accomplished.

President Brown, Elder Hinckley (center), Sisters Suntay and Cahoucum of the Luzon District (left), Ivan Teucher, president of the Luzon District, Keith E. Garner, president of the Southern Far East Mission, and Elder Dale Duke.

Assurances were obtained from the government that missionaries would be granted visas. Therefore, on the early morning of May 28, 1961, a small Latter-day Saint group led by Elder Gordon B. Hinckley gathered on the grounds of the American Battle Memorial Cemetery at Fort Bonifacio (William McKinley) to officially initiate missionary work.

Elder Hinckley recorded the solemnity of that occasion in his diary in these words:

> Arose at 4:30 a.m. to go out to the American War Memorial Cemetery on the outskirts of Manila for a sunrise service. This service had been planned as an occasion to dedicate the Philippines for the preaching of the gospel. When I told them that the islands had been dedicated on August 21, 1955, by President Joseph Fielding Smith, they were greatly surprised. However, it was determined to go forward with the meeting since word had spread among the members of the Church in the Philippines that the service would be held.
>
> This cemetery is the most beautiful place I have seen in the Philippines, also one of the most tragic. Here are buried 17,168 war dead and on the walls are inscribed the names of an additional 36,230 who are missing. Here is told in beautiful

stones and sweeping lawns the tragedy of World War II. As we drove in the gate, there came to my mind the lines that came out of World War I: "In Flanders Field the poppies grow between the crosses row on row."

Here are thousands upon thousands of white crosses marking the final resting place of the war dead.

At this hour of the morning, with the sun rising over the mountains and the sea to the east with golden clouds in the sky, it was a marvelous setting.

Here we met to invoke the blessings of the Lord upon the missionary work in the Philippines. There were in attendance about a hundred members of the Church, including a number who had come by bus from Clark Field. They had left at 3:00 o'clock this morning. The service was brief and beautiful. Surrounded by the tragedy of war, we met in the name of the Prince of Peace. Sister Maxine Grimm had brought the little pump organ that she had carried through the Pacific and had played as she, with the Red Cross, moved in behind our advancing forces from Borneo up into the Philippines into the Ryukyuan Islands into Japan.

Following an opening song and prayer, she told of the first Latter-day Saint services held in the Philippines. She described how our servicemen would get together wherever they stopped. It was a touching story. Sister Grimm told of a Philippine woman who had been baptized here, but we have no record of her. She was the first woman baptized in the Philippines. I think we should try to find her.

We then called on Brother David Lagman, who was the first man baptized in the Philippines. He is now an ordained elder. He gave his testimony, recounting how some years ago he came across an old copy of the *Reader's Digest* which contained an abridgement of "Children of God." He was impressed with the thought that Joseph Smith was claimed to be a prophet. His interest grew, but he could find nothing more concerning the Mormons. Some years passed, and then he got a job working at Clark Field. There he met a member of the Church by the name of Larson, who taught him the gospel and baptized him.

David Lagman (back center), the first known Filipino man baptized, is shown here with his family and President Robert S. Taylor (left) and Elder Gordon B. Hinckley (right) standing by Ping Bachelor, who awaits baptism. April, 1961.

I then spoke and offered a special prayer invoking the blessings of the Lord upon our labors here. We had a musical number from a group at Clark Field and a concluding number from the choir with a brief word of benediction. President Robert S. Taylor conducted the services. It was an inspirational meeting, and one that I shall never forget.

One week after this service the first four missionaries arrived: Elders Ray Goodson, Harry Murray, Kent Lowe, and Nestor Ledesma. This number was increased to eight in 1962, twenty-two in 1963, thirty-two in 1964, forty in 1965, and about sixty in 1966.

In October, 1962, President Jay A. Quealy, Jr., became president of the Southern Far East Mission, and under his leadership in 1963 there were 232 baptisms by twenty-two missionaries in the Philippines. By the end of 1964, there were 263 baptisms and thirty-two missionaries.

Convert baptisms and total Church membership have grown tremendously in the Philippine Islands since the arrival of the first missionaries. Unlike other fields in East Asia there were not significant numbers of baptisms of natives before that time. However, when the missionaries arrived in 1962 there were approximately two hundred and fifty members of the Church in the Philippines, almost entirely American servicemen. By the end of 1963 the membership rose to four hundred fifty, to eight hundred in 1964, to thirteen hundred fifty in 1965, and very close to two thousand at the end of 1966. The harvest in the Philippine Islands has been the most dramatic of any of the Asian missions.

In February of 1964 a building site with a land area of about 5,000 square meters was acquired in a choice area of Makati, Rizal, near Manila. Groundbreaking ceremonies were held on September 6, 1964, with E. M. Grimm and Lester Tracy, supervisor and builder, turning the first shovels of dirt to signal the start of construction.

By February, 1965, the Luzon District was able to send out its first full-time Filipino missionaries to the Hawaii Mission: Elders Catalino Brocka, an early convert of the Manila Branch, and Emiliano Antonio, Jr., of the Quezon City Branch.

Philippines Chapel at Makati, Risal, dedicated October 23, 1966.

On February 28, 1965, the Filipino Saints earned the distinction of having the first elders quorum in the Southern Far East Mission organized among their people.

When President Quealy was released as president of the Southern Far East Mission in the summer of 1965, forty-six missionaries were laboring in the Philippines; two were laboring in San Fernando in Panpanga Province, two-thirds of the way between Manila and Clark Air Force Base; two were in Angeles, immediately outside the gates of Clark Air Force Base; two were in Baguio, a summer resort area north of Clark Air Base; and two were in Cavite, a city connected with Sangley Navel Air Base, just across the bay from Manila. Thus the branches of the Church were dependencies or outgrowths of specific American servicemen's installations and were part of one district—Luzon.

This district was presided over by an American, President Joseph Cook, a Navy doctor. His counselors were Elder Clifford Huntington, a missionary, and Brother Lacanienta, a local Filipino member. Their district council was composed of local and foreign brethren. All branches were presided over by brethren other than missionaries. Americans presided over the Clark, Subic, and Cavite branches, while Filipinos presided over the San Fernando, Manila, Quezon City, and Baguio branches.

The Philippines Mission

The Philippines Mission of the Church was officially organized on August 21, 1967, when President and Sister Paul S. Rose of Murray, Utah, arrived in Manila to direct its affairs. At that time there were seventy full-time foreign missionaries laboring in ten areas of the country.

By late 1969, after two years of labor, the membership was almost doubled, to a total of five thousand; one thousand of these were added in the first eight months of that year. By December, 1969, there were 167 missionaries in the mission, four of whom were full-time Filipino elders. There were also eleven part-time local missionaries.

The Philippines Mission has thirty-six organized groups and branches, divided into two districts:

1. *The Northern Philippine District,* in northern Luzon, has eight branches and three groups. These include San Fernando, Subic Bay, Angeles (also Clark Air Base), San Antonio, Tarlac, Cabantuan, Dagupan, Baguio, and Ladag.

2. *The Central Philippine District,* embracing Manila and the southern islands, includes eleven branches and fourteen groups. There are seven branches in the immediate Manila area: Manila, Makati, Quezon City, Santa Mesa, Caloocan, and Marikina-Pasig. The others are Lemery-Taal, San Pablo, Batangas, Cavite, Los Banos, Lucena, Naga, Legaspi, Talloban, Bacolod, Iloilo, Cebu, Dumaguete, Batuan, Ozamiz, Cagayan de Oro, Iligan, David, and General Cantos (Dadiangas).

About two-thirds of the district and branch leaders are Filipino brethren and the rest are foreigners. In the present district leadership are three local leaders and three foreigners. Both counselors to the mission president are Filipinos.

At the end of 1969 the Church owned only two buildings in the Philippine Islands: the mission home and the lovely Makati Chapel. However, plans were underway for the construction of a new two-branch chapel in Quezon City.

As in all newly established and vibrant missions throughout the world, President Rose has given much attention to the training of local leadership in the Philippines. One reason for his success has been the common use of English as a native language there, an advantage not generally enjoyed by the other missions of the Church in Asia. Communication between the leadership in Salt Lake City and the local membership in the Philippines is thus more effective than elsewhere in that part of the world. Of course, the Christian background of many of the people of that country has also proved beneficial.

VII

Beginnings in THAILAND

Beginnings in THAILAND

Thirteen Mormon elders boarded the ship *Monsoon* at San Francisco en route to mission assignments in southern Asia. Nine were headed for India and four for Siam (present-day Thailand). They arrived in Calcutta on April 26, 1853. These four were Chauncey W. West, Elam Luddington, Benjamin F. Dewey, and Levi Savage. Because of war between the Burmese government and the East India Company (which in effect was an arm of the British government in Asia), their passage from Calcutta to Bangkok was delayed. Therefore, Elders West and Dewey were reassigned to Ceylon.

Elders Luddington and Savage tried to reach Siam via Rangoon, Burma, but their ship sprung a leak and they had to return to Calcutta. However, on August 10, 1853, they finally arrived in Rangoon aboard this same ship. According to their report, they felt "penniless and alone; strangers in a foreign land, [where there was] nothing but war and bloodshed, unacquainted with the language, a kingdom of gross darkness." They were met in Burma by a prominent new convert, Matthew McCune (whose son Alfred W. McCune later gave a $250,000 mansion to the Church for the creation of the McCune School of Music).

Of the four elders originally assigned to Siam, only Elder Luddington reached that country. He arrived alone on April 6, 1854, and spent four months and five days in Bangkok. He was stoned twice. He was once administered poison. But he was once kindly treated by a Moslem king. He worked among foreigners in Siam, and his only baptisms were Captain James Trail and wife, at night, on April 9, 1854. But through all his varied adventures, Elder Luddington was a persistent and faithful missionary to the last day of his mission. Because he was a man of such incomparable fortitude, his experience in the mission field ranks among the greatest of the early missionaries of the Church.

A startling but revealing letter written shortly after Elder Luddington arrived in "The Kingdom of Siam" dramatizes his situation:

> June 1, 1854
>
> I am situated in an insalubrious clime, among a few friends and surrounded by many foes, who seek to contaminate and overthrow every righteous principle, and imitate the natives in nudity, debauchery, enebriety, etc.
>
> I arrived here on the first day of your annual conference, on the 6th day of April, a stranger and alone, in an uncivilized country.
>
> I visited one of their festivals a few days ago. I was cautioned to go armed, as they are a set of wild barbarians, outlaws; they would as soon take your life as to look at you. I had a view of heathen scenery, it was picturesque; fire works, Burmese dancing, masks and Indian paintings, in true Asiatic style.
>
> A large portion of the populace are Chinese, skilled in all manner of hypocrisy, and there are thousands of sons of Ishmael, and of different tribes and nations of the antipodes of the earth.
>
> I have delivered one lecture every Sabbath since my arrival in Bangkok; some eight or ten Europeans generally attend. I am trying to learn the native language; it no doubt will take me from one to two years; the reverends say five. Mr. Dilsbery, now on his way back to Ohio, I think, has studied the language seven years, and can't preach yet in Siamese. I will keep digging till you all say enough, and then if you see fit to call me home I shall be truly in heaven and happy in the extreme; or if you say "Spend your days in Father India," it shall be even so; not my will, but my heavenly Father's be done.
>
> Utah is a land of peace; India is Hell, and the smoke of her torment gets thicker and thicker. The whole earth is defiled with broken covenants, and men and women are full of abominations.
>
> Elder Elam Luddington[1]

On his return ocean voyage to America at the end of his mission, he experienced a typhoon, a mutiny, a fire at sea, and a famine at sea. Then finally, almost surprisingly, he reached San Francisco safely June 27, 1855.[2]

---

[1]Letter written to Elder George Wallace, *Deseret News*, Thursday, November 16, 1854.

[2]Cf. Robert C. Patch, *An Historical Overview of the Missionary Activities of the Church of Jesus Christ of Latter-day Saints in Continental Asia* (Brigham Young University, M.A. Thesis, 1949), pp. 89-90.

The Dedication of Thailand

More than a century of virtual revolution would transpire before full-time missionaries of the Church would return to the kingdom of Thailand following World War II. During that time the Thai court often encouraged contact with foreign people, but Thailand remained the only country in South and Southeast Asia that was never colonized by a European power.

Japan's defeat at the end of World War II has been followed by an era of increasingly close relations with the United States, and no doubt the Vietnam war has also helped prepare the way for the return of the Mormon missionaries and the dedication of Thailand for the preaching of the gospel.

At 6:30 a.m. on the morning of November 2, 1966, Elder Gordon B. Hinckley of the Council of the Twelve, President Marion D. Hanks of the First Council of Seventy, President Keith E. Garner of the Southern Far East Mission, and a small group of Latter-day Saints from the Bangkok Servicemen's Branch assembled in Bangkok's Lumpini Park for the dedication of the land of Thailand for the preaching of the gospel. Brother Hinckley's prayer of dedication is as follows:

> Our Father and our God, we come unto thee in the name of thy Son, Jesus Christ, with grateful hearts this beautiful morning. We are thankful, Father, for the purpose for which we are met, to turn the key to the preaching of the gospel in this ancient land of Thailand.
>
> Our hearts are full of gratitude unto thee for the gift of thy Son, the Lord Jesus Christ, and for the gift of his life, which has made possible eternal life for all who will hearken unto his teachings. We thank thee for the light of the gospel restored in this dispensation of time, for thy coming and the coming of thy Son to the boy Joseph Smith, and for thy declaration unto him. We thank thee for the coming of heavenly messengers thereafter with a bestowal of keys and authority, bringing to pass a restoration of all of previous dispensations for the blessing of thy children throughout the earth. We thank thee, Father, for faithful servants, missionaries who in times past gathered our forebears from among the nations of the earth and for the glorious blessings of the gospel which have come to us because of their faith. We thank thee for those who are abroad in the earth today preaching the restored gospel. We pray thy blessings upon them wherever they may be, that their labors may be fruitful and that their joy may be great.

This morning we are particularly grateful for those of thy Church who have come to this land in the service of the United States and who, while so serving, have gathered together frequently to bear testimony one to another and to increase their faith in thee. As they have worshipped thee, there has come into their hearts a desire to share that which they have with others. We thank thee for their great desire that this land be opened to missionary endeavor.

And now, our Father, in the authority of the Holy Priesthood, even the authority of the Holy Apostleship in us vested, we dedicate and consecrate this land of Thailand, this ancient kingdom of Siam, to the preaching of the everlasting gospel, even the restored gospel of the Lord Jesus Christ.

We pray that thy Spirit may rest upon this land and this nation. Soften the hearts of the people that they may listen with understanding and accept the truth. Bless those who shall teach thy gospel, the missionaries who will be sent here—bless them with thy holy spirit and love for the people among whom they labor. Loosen their tongues that they shall speak the language of the people, and bless them that they shall be effective in proclaiming thy word; and may there be many, Father, yea, thousands and tens of thousands, who will hearken to their message. Open the way before thy servants that the blessings of thy work and thy word may come to the people of this land, that they may draw near unto thee and that there may be fulfilled here the revealed purposes for which thy gospel has been restored in this dispensation, namely, that every man might speak in the name of God, the Lord, even the Savior of the world; that faith also might increase in the earth; that thine everlasting covenant might be established; and that the fulness of thy gospel might be proclaimed by the weak and the simple unto the ends of the world, and before kings and rulers, that they might come to understanding.

Father in heaven, pour out thy spirit upon this land. Soften the hearts of the people. Take from them the elements of cruelty and meanness which have troubled so many in the past. Increase their love one for another, and may the bonds of brotherhood and affection be strengthened among them. May they grow in leadership in thy kingdom as they partake of the blessings of thy glorious truth.

Holy Father, we pray that thou wilt bless those who govern this nation that they may be men of judgment and understanding, of goodness and virtue, that the lives of the citizens of the land may be blessed. Touch the hearts of these rulers that they may be kindly to thy servants, that the way may be opened without difficulty that thy servants may travel here in the coming years to preach thy word and find a friendly reception, not only at the hands of the people but at the hands of those who stand in positions of government. Open the way, Father, that properties may be found, that houses of worship may be established, that thy word may be taught and instruction given to all who will hear.

Now, Holy Father, as we gather this morning we sustain before thee thy anointed servant, the prophet of this day, under whose authority we exercise the keys of the apostleship in dedicating this land. We pray likewise for all who stand in positions of responsibility in thy kingdom wherever they may be. And we invoke upon this land and this nation the blessings of peace and pray that thou wilt overrule throughout the realm of Southeast Asia, that some solution may be found to the terrible conflict which is presently bringing so much suffering and oppression to the peoples of this part of the earth.

Holy Father, we acknowledge before thee our love for thee and our love for thy Son. We acknowledge thee as the God of the heavens, the Creator and ruler of the universe, our Father. We acknowledge before thee thy beloved Son as our Savior and Redeemer and·express unto thee and unto him our love for him. Accept our gratitude, accept of this dedication, accept of our faith, we ask as we rededicate ourselves to thy holy service and invoke thy blessing upon that which we here do and upon those who shall follow us in thy ministry, in the name of thy Son, Jesus Christ. Amen.

This dedicatory service marked the beginning of a two-year struggle through government channels to incorporate the Church in Thailand. Upon receiving approval from the First Presidency, and under the direction of President Keith B. Garner of the Southern Far East Mission, a vanguard of elders arrived in Bangkok on February 2, 1968. These were: Peter W. Basker, Honolulu, Hawaii; Craig G. Christensen[3], Santa Barbara, California; L. Carl Hansen, Rexburg, Idaho; Alan H. Hess, Ogden, Utah; Larry R. White, Grant's Pass, Oregon; Robert W. Winegar, Layton, Utah. With the exception of Elder Hess, who had been transferred from Hong Kong, all of the elders had previously labored in the Taiwan Zone of the Southern Far East Mission. A home to serve as living quarters for the elders was secured in the Bangkok section of Bangkok on Sukumvit Road. On Monday, February 5, President Garner returned to the mission headquarters in Hong Kong, leaving the missionaries under the direction of District Leader Christensen, with Glen L. Wilcox of the Bangkok Branch as adviser.

The mission president's instructions were short and expli-

---

[3]The story of Church beginnings in Thailand, on the following pages, was kindly provided by Craig Christensen.

cit: learn the Thai language and arrange to have the six missionary discussions translated. At the date of their arrival, there was no Church literature in the Thai language; not even the name of the Church had been translated. Feeling at a loss and strange in metropolitan Bangkok, the elders relied much on fasting and prayer for guidance. Within one week a translator for the six discussions had been employed and a language school with Thai instructors had been located for the elders to attend. At the language school, the elders underwent three weeks of intensive instruction in the Thai language. In the evenings, time was utilized by tracting in the *farang* (foreign) areas of the city. The reaction of most Occidentals to the undertaking ranged from scorn to pity. "Your failure is assured," the elders were told. "The Thais have a religion that is perfectly suited to them. Don't try to change a contented people with your western religion." The thrust of these opinions was amplified when it was learned that the first Protestant missionaries in Thailand had labored for 37 years before baptizing their first convert. Only in recent years had the entire Bible been available in a Thai translation, and even that still had many flaws. According to estimates, 97 percent of Thailand is Buddhist, with the remaining portion divided among the Moslems, Catholics, Protestants, and Hindus.

The first crucial weeks were accompanied with a special blessing: a young Thai man, Anan Eldredge, who had been adopted by an American Latter-day Saint family living in Thailand and was subsequently baptized, was sent to live with the elders in order to help them in their study of the Thai language. With his help, the elders were able to conduct the first service entirely in the Thai language a mere five weeks after their arrival in Thailand. Elder Alan Hess conducted the meeting, and Brother Anan presented the lesson. Six Thai investigators were present.

The pressures and frustrations of the initial weeks were made more endurable through the meeting of a very special individual. With the help of Dr. Gordon H. Flammer of the Bangkok Branch, the elders were introduced to a bright Thai gentleman and his wife: Boonepluke and Rabiab Klaophin. Mr.

Boonepluke (Thais use the first name almost exclusively) was employed at the school where Dr. Flammer taught and had expressed interest in the Church because of his observation of the habits and characteristics of the Church members. Mr. Boonepluke had taught himself English to communicate on a fairly technical level, so the missionaries began to teach him the six discussions in English, and he, in turn, would translate for his wife.

Without exception, these meetings were spiritual experiences. Mr. Boonepluke's desire to learn the gospel was something extremely rare. He literally memorized each point in the discussions and made certain he had thoroughly digested the material in each lesson before proceeding to the next. He understood the significance of prayer and made certain that his family had daily prayers. He became a regular participant at the weekly meetings held in the elders' home, even though attendance meant a one-hour motorcycle ride with his wife and two children through the crowded streets of Bangkok. Not only that, but his punctuality in a land where time is considered only in terms of "early" and "late" was truly commendable.

At length, Brother Boonepluke and his wife were challenged to be baptized. A Thai man who rejects Buddhism is looked upon as something of a traitor, because Buddhism and the Thai government are inextricably related historically, ceremonially, and philosophically. Such a person becomes a social outcast in many circles, and is almost certain to bring disgrace upon his family. Nevertheless, after much personal prayer and counsel from the missionaries, Brother Boonepluke and his wife were baptized and confirmed members of the Church on Saturday, May 15, 1968.

There are two other converts whose roles in the establishment of the Church in Thailand should be mentioned. Brother Prasong Sriveses, who was employed by the Thailand District president, Eugene P. Till, listened to the six discussions in "pidgin" Thai (as then spoken by the elders) with a degree of comprehension that can only be explained as a gift of the Holy Ghost. At an exceptionally spiritual baptismal service on

June 12, 1968, Brother Prasong was baptized, and the following week he was ordained a priest and set apart as a counselor
in the Sunday School superintendency.

A few weeks after arriving in Bangkok, two of the elders
met an extraordinary lady, Mrs. Srilaksanaa. Of noble ancestry,
she was well educated and had traveled extensively. She con-
sented to listen to the discussions and did so with sincerity
and intense interest. Through prayer and study of the Book of
Mormon, she gained a fervent testimony and, with her two
daughters, was baptized on July 4. Since that time, her eloquence and strong testimony have been invaluable in the conversion of other Thai people. She has served the Church as
teacher of an investigators class and has assisted often in
translation work.

In June, 1968, President Garner was in Bangkok in con-
junction with a district conference and was inspired to send
two elders to the city of Nakorn Rajasima, better known as
Korat, to begin missionary work there. Elder Christensen and
Elder Scott E. Blickenstaff (who, with Elder Larry Blake, had
arrived late in May) were chosen, and they arrived in Korat
on June 21. A home was secured, and the following week
regular Sunday meetings were started. Fortunately, Brother
Anan Eldredge and his family were then living in Korat, and
he was again invaluable in starting the work there. While
Korat is the third largest city in Thailand, in comparison
with Bangkok it is only a village, with a population of about
75,000. But from the beginning there was a special spirit
there, and the hand of the Lord was evident countless times
in locating and converting those souls whom he had prepared
to receive the gospel. In a short time, the Korat group had
about 30 in regular attendance, and baptismal services were
held monthly. The converts were from all walks of life: students,
military men, common laborers, and two former Protestant
ministers. The circumstances of their conversions were almost
without exception dramatic and miraculous. In a few months
it was necessary to find a larger meeting place.

From the outset the American elders have been impressed
with the people of Thailand, whose population of 34 million

is composed primarily of Thai stock. They have reported that their warmth and sincerity are unmatched anywhere, that they are quick to make friends and are generally humble and content with their lives, and that they are quick to smile and slow to anger. The elders say that it would not be difficult for one who is acquainted with the Polynesian temperament to understand the Thais.

Taking the above characteristics into consideration, work in Thailand is looked upon as a delightful experience. However, it must be added that the Thais are tolerant of religions to an unnerving degree, thus rendering attempts to teach or impose any *one* set of beliefs often unfruitful. This particular difficulty will likely be unsettling to missionaries in Thailand for years to come.

In July, 1968, President Keith E. Garner was released as president of the Southern Far East Mission, and W. Brent Hardy was sent apart as the new mission president. Under the direction of President Hardy, the elders then laboring in Bangkok were assigned to revise and correct the existing translations of the six missionary lessons. This proved to be a ponderous task, for the native Thai translators they hired were faced with two major problems: (1) they were not familiar with the Church terminology and doctrine; and (2) the Thai language makes no provision for Christian concepts, i.e. "Savior" must be translated "the Holy One who helps." To date, no suitable equivalent for the word "priesthood" has been discovered or coined. It is a credit to those elders that after studying the Thai language a mere six months, they were able to compile a correct and suitable translation of the six discussions that is still in use today.

Thus, after only eight months in Thailand, the Church was established in two cities, the six missionary discussions had been translated correctly, and a good translation of "Joseph Smith's Testimony" was ready to go to press. To the elders who took part in this task, progress at times seemed painfully slow; but in retrospect, their achievements were nothing short of miraculous.

In December, 1968, Elder Ezra Taft Benson of the Council

of the Twelve visited Bangkok to attend a quarterly district conference. During his visit, he was granted an audience with the King of Thailand and presented him with a Book of Mormon and a copy of *Joseph Smith's Testimony* printed in the Thai language.

During the same district conference, President Hardy instructed two sets of elders to travel throughout different cities in northern Thailand to determine which of those cities might be suitable for missionary work. Elders Alan Hess and Larry White were assigned to the northwest provinces and Elders Craig Christensen and Troy Corriveau to the northeast provinces. Their experiences and findings on these trips were helpful in deciding which cities would be opened for missionary endeavors. In particular, the experiences of Elder Hess and Elder White are of interest to the Church scholar as well as the anthropologist.

In the northern provinces of Thailand dwell several hill tribes whose culture, language, and traditions differ markedly from the Thais who inhabit the lowlands. Elders Hess and White had heard of a tape recording that described some of these traditions. Regarding the tape, the following is taken from Elder Hess's journal:

> After a while we decided to go in search of the people who sold the Karen hill tribe music tapes. All seemed to go without a hitch. The post office gave us the address of the post office box number we had received. When we got to the place, we found it to be the Baptist Mission. They have done extensive work among the hill tribes. They were quite curious as to why we wanted the tape, but they sold it to us anyway. Later we went into a tape recording shop and played it. This narrator told how the Karens have a legend about a golden book which was given to their forefathers. They say that they lost this "Book of Life" through negligence. They also say that some white men will bring it to them again. Here is the narration as taken from that tape: "The story of the Golden Book of Life has a large place in the traditions of the Karens. After Creation, God sojourned with man for a while, then returned to heaven to the company of His youngest son, a white man. Upon arriving in heaven, God gave the white man three books of life, one each for his children on earth. The books were delivered, and the white brother took his leave to the west, promising to pay a return visit someday. However, the Karen Indians soon lost their golden book through negligence

and began wandering the pathway of animistic fears. With fervent expectation and hope, the Karen looks for the coming again of his white brothers with the Golden Book of Life." This longing helped open the way for early Christian missionaries. It is little wonder that the Bible has become the touchstone of the Karen Church and its faith.

It is pure speculation, but nonetheless intriguing to consider the effect that the Book of Mormon might have on a people with such legends. Many of the Thai people have a common heritage with these hill tribes, in spite of the fact that they differ greatly today.

The following is a translation of a chant that has been handed down through the centuries among these hill tribes:

The old men tell us, "Children remember this:
Remember that the white foreigner will return the Golden Book.
When that happens, take the book, and take care of it.
If you don't it'll be lost, and then there will be no hope at all.
We're old, it's too late for us, but you'll be there.
Watch the sea for the big ship.
Where the waves beat themselves white,
Watch for the white man's ship.
They'll have the golden book.
Take it."

Continuing from Elder Hess's journal:

Upon arrival in Chiang Mai we were speaking with some of the taxi drivers and one of them gave us the name of a Mr. Thompson, who was from the Karen tribe, but was taken when just a child and brought up by Baptist missionaries. He works in a local bank and is active in the Baptist Church. The Lord was really with us in that almost as soon as we arrived back at the hotel, one of the workers there came to our door, and even before we asked she said that she knew where Mr. Thompson lived and offered to take us there. We went with this little lady on a bus and up a road on the other end of town that would have been almost impossible for us to find on our own. Mr. Thompson received us most kindly, and upon request, related the tribe legend to us a little bit differently than we had heard it before. He said there was a gold book and a silver book which had been lost. The Baptists had been teaching that one book was the Bible and one was the hymn book. We told him about Joseph Smith, the gold plates, and the story of the Book of Mormon. He seemed impressed, but didn't really understand the import. But he did agree to pray about it. And we told him we would go to his bank the following day and take him a Book of Mormon.

Further information regarding these hill tribes is beyond the scope of this book. The portion that has been presented is intended to convey the spirit of the missionary work in Thailand rather than be source material for the scholar. Such a task must be reserved for much more thorough research.

It is too early to appraise results of missionary beginnings in Thailand. Yet the consensus of the first elders to work in that land is aptly expressed by these words of Elder Craig Christensen:

> I cannot restrain a note of optimism, admittedly—though not apologetically—emotional: The Lord has a great purpose in sending missionaries in Thailand. Those saints who witnessed the incipient struggles and subsequent successes of the work there will attest to that fact. There is every reason to believe that the words of Elder Hinckley in his dedicatory prayer will be fulfilled: that thousands and tens of thousands of Thai people will one day become members of The Church of Jesus Christ of Latter-day Saints.

VIII

The dedication of VIETNAM

The dedication of VIETNAM

Latter-day Saint missionaries have not yet been sent to the war-torn country of Vietnam, but it has been dedicated for the preaching of the gospel. The dedicatory prayer was offered by Elder Gordon B. Hinckley of the Council of the Twelve in Saigon, South Vietnam, Sunday, October 30, 1966. This was a part of a service held in the roof garden room of the Caravelle Hotel in the heart of Saigon. Because of war conditions it was deemed inadvisable to hold the service in a park or to seek a hill on the outskirts of the city. The roof of the hotel was accordingly chosen.

Elder Hinckley, with President Marion D. Hanks of the First Council of Seventy and President Keith E. Garner of the Southern Far East Mission, conducted district conferences in Da Nang, Nha Trang, and Saigon on Saturday and Sunday, October 29 and 30, and the following dedicatory prayer was offered at the conclusion of the conference held in Saigon. Two hundred and five members of the Church attended.

O God, our Eternal Father, with humble hearts we meet before Thee this day in this land of South Vietnam, a land which presently is torn by war, destruction, and dissension. We meet in the name of thy Son, the Lord Jesus Christ, the Prince of Peace, to invoke thy special blessing. We are grateful, Father, for the land of America, from which most of us have come, and for the cause of human liberty which was established there under a constitution written by those whom thou raised up unto this very purpose. We are grateful for the restoration of the gospel of the Lord Jesus Christ in that land, and for its spread from there to many other lands and to many other places.

We have seen in other parts of Asia the manner in which thou hast turned the hand and the work of the adversary to the good and the blessing of many of thy children. And now we call

In Saigon for the dedication of Vietnam and Thailand: left to right, Major Allen C. Rozsa, Elders Marion D. Hanks and Gordon B. Hinckley, supervisors of the Oriental missions, and Keith E. Garner, president of the Southern Far East Mission. Vietnam was dedicated October 30, 1966, and Thailand, November 2, 1966.

upon thee at this time that thou wilt similarly pour out thy spirit upon this land. We plead with thee, our Father and our God, that thou wilt touch the hearts of the leaders of those people who war one against another, with a spirit of understanding, a recognition of the fact that all men are sons of thine and therefore brothers, and implant in each a desire to labor for a settlement of the great conflict which rages over this land, a settlement which will be honorable and one which will promote the cause of liberty and justice and which will guarantee the agency of those who love freedom. Overrule, Father, that those who would stifle agency and liberty may be stopped in their evil designs, that righteousness may reign, and that those who live in this beautiful land may be free to follow honorable pursuits without trouble, without hindrance, without injury, and without compulsion.

Holy Father, many good men holding thy priesthood have come to this land incident to the war. While here they have sought to establish thy divine work in this part of the world. They have shared the gospel of thy Son with their associates, their fellow Americans, and with the Vietnamese people. With gratitude we have witnessed the baptism of a number of these people. And so we feel it expedient at this time, under the authority given us by thy prophet, him whom thou hast anointed and appointed to stand at the head of thy work in this day, to dedicate this land and invoke thy blessings upon it.

We accordingly come before thee in the exercise of the Holy Priesthood, and in the authority of the Holy Apostleship in us vested we dedicate and consecrate this land of South Vietnam for the preaching of the gospel of the Lord Jesus Christ as restored through the Prophet Joseph Smith. May there from this time forward, Father, come upon this land an added measure of thy holy spirit to touch the hearts of the people and the rulers thereof. May they open their hearts to the teaching of the truth and be receptive to the gospel of thy Son. May those who have these blessings feel a new urge in their hearts to share with others the great gifts and powers and authority which are theirs, which have come from thee, that many may be the partakers of these choice gifts.

Father, again we pray for the land that peace may be established, that righteousness may prevail; that this nation may take its place among the peoples of the earth as a freedom-loving nation established on principles of divine liberty; that thy children may grow in righteousness, in goodness, and in harmonious relationships one with another. Prosper the works of those who seek to serve thee. Hasten the day when the noise of battle may cease and there may grow again a love and understanding and appreciation one for another among the citizens of this part of the earth.

Open the way for the coming of missionaries and make their labors fruitful of great and everlasting good in the lives of the people.

To this end we seek thy blessing this holy day as we bow before thee and acknowledge with thankful hearts thy goodness unto us. As we thus dedicate this land and this nation for the preaching of thy word, we rededicate ourselves to thy service, all of which we do in the name of our Redeemer, the Lord Jesus Christ. Amen.

Later, in a general conference address, Elder Hinckley spoke eloquently, prophetically, of war-torn Vietnam:

I make no defense of . . . war from this pulpit. I seek only to call your attention to that silver thread, small but radiant with hope, shining through the dark tapestry of war—namely, the establishment of a bridgehead, small and frail now; but which somehow under the mysterious ways of God, will be strengthened, and from which someday shall spring forth a great work affecting for good the lives of large numbers of our Father's children who live in that part of the world. Of that I have certain faith.

I have seen a prototype of what will happen as I have witnessed the development of this work in others of the ancient nations of Asia—in Korea, in Taiwan, in Okinawa, in the Philippines, and in Japan, where altogether now we have more than 25,000 Latter-day Saints.

This marvelous membership is the sweet fruit of seed once planted in dark years of war and in the troubled days immediately following, when good men of the priesthood, both civilian and military, through the example of their lives and the inspiration of their precepts, laid a foundation on which a great work has been established.[1]

---

[1]From an address delivered at general conference in Salt Lake City in April, 1968. See *Conference Report*, April, 1968, p. 24.

IX

INDIA

INDIA

> *. . . there is nothing more heroic in our Church annals than the labors and sufferings of these brethren of the missions of India.*
>
> Brigham H. Roberts[1]

Mormon missionary work expanded into India during the mid-nineteenth century, arising naturally from British colonization there. English members of the Church serving in the armed forces of their country in various parts of India made repeated requests for pamphlets, scriptures, and missionaries from Church authorities in London. Thus began one of the most fascinating Church encounters in Asia. It led to the establishment of the "East India Mission," which was officially opened in 1851 with the arrival of Elder Joseph Richards from England.[2]

Elder Richards baptized several foreigners in India, the most important of whom were James Patric Meik and family, Maurice White, and Matthew McCune and family. The Meiks and McCunes served the Church faithfully in Calcutta and Rangoon. (It is interesting to note that a great-grandson of Matthew McCune, Jay A. Quealy, Jr., was called to be president of the Southern Far East Mission in 1962 and that India was placed under his charge.) Elder Richards was later joined by Elder William Willes; thereafter they carried the gospel to Agra, site of the great Taj Mahal, and to the Upper Provinces. In April, 1853, these two elders were joined by thirteen

---

[1]*A Comprehensive History of the Church,* Vol. 4, pp. 72-73.

[2]R. Lanier Britsch of Brigham Young University covers this early India missionary work in detail in his M.A. thesis, *A History of the Missionary Activities of The Church of Jesus Christ of Latter-day Saints in India, 1849-1856,* from which the basic information presented here is taken.

missionaries from America, four of whom were assigned to Siam. Thus the total number of assigned missionaries sent to the East India Mission was fifteen. Although Elders Meik and McCune served as missionaries, they were actually local converts.

During the fall of 1854, the elders suffered great discouragement and began thinking of going home. They had reason. Elder Robert Skelton, the last of the foreign missionaries to return home, stated that there were only about sixty-one members in India and Burma at the time of his departure in May, 1856. Eleven others had immigrated to the Salt Lake Valley. Yet earlier, Elder Willes, who had performed more baptisms than any elder during his mission, had established a branch of about three hundred members, including natives of the country. This number had quickly dwindled when converts learned that they would not receive cash for their membership in the Church, as apparently was the practice among other Christian mission groups at the time.

It was apparent that conditions in India were not favorable for missionary work during those five years the Mormon elders were actively laboring there. Apostasy was a common problem among the European converts in India as well as the natives.

The missionaries sought to teach the natives but failed primarily because they could not speak to them. They attempted to learn Burmese, Hindustani, Tamil, Telegoo, and Maratha, but none of them ever gained mastery.

Then, of course, there was the larger problem of local culture—including a system of rigid social distinctions, and a mystifying jungle of cults, festivals, and taboos.

Another serious problem was the lack of specific guidelines for the missionaries. Although their field of labor was called "the East India Mission," it never had an appointed president except for a brief time when the group decided that Elder Nathaniel Vary Jones should officiate as such. The elders were entirely free to change stations at will and to work wherever they felt they might find success. Professor R. Lanier Britsch, in his study of the early India missionary work, has concluded:

Because the European population would not listen to their message, the elders turned to the native people. Then because the native people would not listen or could not understand, the elders returned home.

India and the Church Today

As of 1970 there are no Mormon missionaries in India. That great land has never been dedicated for the preaching of the restored gospel, and The Church of Jesus Christ of Latter-day Saints has yet to establish an organized missionary program there, although elders have on occasion been sent to India on special short-term assignments by the president of the Southern Far East Mission. Several stalwart souls have been baptized since World War II. Illustrative of these, and suggestive of the enormous challenges facing the Church in that country, is the case of Paul Thiruthuvodoss of Coimbatore, South India. His story, recounted here, comes from the personal diary of Elder Gordon B. Hinckley of the Council of the Twelve.

Saturday, December 12, 1964
Flight to Coimbatore

We had a good flight to Bangalore. Seated immediately behind me was an elderly Indian who looked very much like Mahatma Gandhi. He was dressed in the typical loin cloth, and people were fussing over him. We learned later that he had been one of the leaders of the movement which brought about the separation of India from Britain. He is a much respect elder statesman. He spoke to his associates in a kindly, gracious way in perfect English. I think we were told he is past 80.

We came down to Bangalore, where the weather was pleasant. This is a city 3,927 feet above sea level. The sun was shining brightly but in the shade it was delightful. Preparations were being made for a great affair at the airport to celebrate the manufacture of the first of a new jet trainer fighter plane being built in India under Russian direction. They were to have the inaugural ceremonies for this plane, and great crowds were gathering at the field as we took off.

We arrived in Coimbatore without incident and were there met by Paul Thiruthuvodoss, the man who has asked for baptism. With him was a friend named Job, whose last name I do not recall.

This good man (Paul Thiruthuvodoss), out of his meager earnings, has built a school for underprivileged children. He has two little buildings that were good for this area. Some 400 students attend the school taught by 10 teachers who are paid by the Indian government.

The Indian government also assists with a little food money and this, with relief supplies from the United States, provides the children each day with a lunch consisting of a porridge made of cornmeal, vegetable oil, and powdered milk.

As we entered the grounds, the children lined up in two lines. They placed garlands of flowers about our necks, gave each of us a lime as a token of friendship, and washed our hands in sandalwood water. We then entered the school, where the children sat on the floor and presented us with a program.

It was an interesting sight to look into their bright and eager faces. Children are the same the world over. They sang and danced and provided us with various types of entertainment.

President Quealy had given them a little organ as his personal contribution to the school. One of the teachers played this with great gusto.

We then visited Paul's home, where we met his wife and three children. He is a graduate of Madras State University in accounting. He is the equivalent of a certified public accountant and has worked for 10 years for the Associated Cement Companies, a big firm here.

He is a fine-looking and intelligent man. He speaks English very well and his grammatical construction is perfect. His choice of words is excellent.

He is a Christian gentleman in the finest sense of the word. With his own funds, he has built the school and helps pay the teachers, as well as taking care of incidental expenses. He asks nothing from the Church. In fact, in our conversations, he stated three or four times he did not ask for any assistance from the Church, but he does wish to be baptized. As we left the school, the children clapped and sang. I felt of the goodness of this man, who has their interest at heart.

I have been so tired because of little sleep and the heat that I have not felt alert. We returned to the hotel and lay down for an hour and went fast asleep. This rest was most refreshing.

After a light dinner, we got in the cars to travel out into a rural section to attend a meeting. Paul and his associates have five meeting places where they hold outdoor meetings among the poor. This has been an unforgettable experience.

We drove about ten miles out of Coimbatore into the rural areas where the dust is thick and people are miserably poor. The men are field hands who earn 30 or 40 cents a day working 12 hours. The women get about 20 cents.

There are many children—11,400,000 born in India each year. As we came into a little opening where there were a few trees, Paul's associates were playing the organ and singing and beating a drum. It was just like a Salvation Army meeting. The people began to gather. Some two or three hundred gathered and sat on the ground. They had taken two cots and put rough blankets on them, and we sat on these.

A hymn was sung which we did not know. It was sung as the Indians sing with their particular type of musical arrangement. President Quealy then offered prayer and Brother Paul interpreted his prayer. I was then called on to speak, and I did so for a few minutes with Paul interpreting. Paul then spoke to them in the Tamil language. He was followed by Job, who gave a regular Pentacostal sermon which we did not understand. Some of the old men seated on the ground in front nodded their heads in approval. The congregation was very reverent.

These were surely the poor of the earth. They appeared to have little or nothing. As we met with them, I thought of Jesus speaking to the multitudes.

The benediction was offered by Brother Robert Evans with Paul translating. We then drove to another meeting in the opposite direction. We were more than an hour late getting there. As we entered a place through dark, narrow, dirty streets, I saw a sight the like of which I have never seen before. A great crowd of people, perhaps 400 of them, were singing in a compound. They had decorated it with paper streamers. A fluorescent light and a gasoline lantern attracted the bugs. Signs reading "welcome" were seen in two or three places. A picture of John F. Kennedy was nailed to a post and another of Nehru. When we drove up the people came over and gathered about us till we could scarcely get out of the cars. These were dirty, hungry, poor people, but they had an eagerness in their eyes that was wonderful to behold. Perhaps 200 children sat on the ground before us with their elders behind them. I spoke briefly through an interpreter, Paul spoke, and Job spoke. We had been so late coming that it was now 9:00, and with so many children present we felt that we should be brief. When we left to go, the people again gathered about the car and took our hands.

We returned to the English Club and had something to eat. My thoughts are greatly troubled over what I have seen. I do not know what we should do. These are earnest people, but they have been schooled in the Pentacostal ways, which are not our ways. Furthermore, the task of working among the poor of India is so great that I do not know where we should start. We certainly need the inspiration of the Lord in whatever action we take here.

I slept wonderfully. We are in this old room with a high ceiling. A frame extends above our bed and from this is suspended a mosquito tent. Our ceiling fan was turning slowly throughout the night. This place is quiet. There is no honking of automobile horns or the noise of traffic. We were in bed by 10:00 and I awoke about 5:30.

I rose to find that there was no hot water. What a boon plenty of hot water is, like so many things we never miss until we are without them.

I earnestly sought the inspiration of the Lord as to whether we should baptize these people. The Quealys later came to our room and we again prayed for the inspiration of the Lord. We then went out to Medukerai to Paul's school. Here we had a wonderful experience. There were about 200 children seated neatly in rows on the floor. At Paul's request, I offered the opening prayer. We sang "We Thank Thee, O God, for a Prophet." That is, we Americans sang it. Our friends sang a hymn in Tamil. We sang two Christmas carols, alternating the verses in English and Tamil. Following a few such exercises, the children went over to the other little buildings and we were left with the adults. Each of us spoke briefly—Sister Quealy, Sister Hinckley, Brother Evans, President Quealy, and I. Brother Quealy and I spoke in a straightforward manner on the events of the restoration. The closing prayer was pronounced by one of the local brethren.

We then went to Brother Paul's home for lunch. We first blessed his baby of a few weeks. I gave the blessing and named him Jacob Kennedy Thiruthuvodoss. I was assisted in this by President Quealy and Brother Evans.

We then sat down to dinner, and I had some misgivings since Paul had said that he was going to give us a real Indian lunch.

We had roast chicken and baked potato. This was Western enough. We then had some Indian food that was terribly hot. We concluded with some gelatin and fruit salad.

Paul had somehow managed to get the cement company's cook and butler to take care of us. While we were eating, his school teachers were seated in another room. When we concluded, we went out into another small room and they came in and sat on the floor and had a different type of dinner. When they were through, he invited the two taxi drivers in to eat.

We then returned to the hotel where I talked with him at length I told him that I felt he was worthy to be baptized. He has read much of our literature and seems to understand the doctrines of the Church thoroughly, but he knows nothing of procedures. I wondered whether we should baptize him and him alone and then leave him here alone. I told him that if we were to baptize him alone and not the others, this might have the effect of dividing his group. I told him that I felt inclined to go home and recommend to the Brethren that we permit two missionaries to come here for a period of months and work with him and his associates, training them in the procedures of the Church, so that if they left they could go forward as an organized branch. I think he would be worthy to be ordained an elder after a few months. He seemed disappointed that we were not inclined to baptize him but said that he felt that this was the wise thing to do and that he would readily accept our judgment. For more than ten years he has wanted to be baptized.

We talked at length about the doctrines of the Church, and he seemed to understand them. However, after attending the meetings last night, I have been greatly worried lest they slip into some kind of Pentacostal method of conducting meetings. They need help in the procedures of the Church, and we have felt that we might do a great injustice by baptizing them and leaving them to drift. He maintained that all of those who attended our Sunday School meeting were thoroughly conversant with the doctrines we discussed.

We suggested that rather than dissipate their energies in going out to hold meetings in the villages, they concentrate on establishing a branch. I think if the missionaries could be here within a month's time, a number of Paul's associates could be baptized and a small branch could be organized with the missionaries presiding. Then within a period of six months Brother Paul could be ordained an elder and could preside over the group, and a decision could be made at that time as to whether we are to extend the proselyting activity or to let them go forward as an organized branch, teaching and bringing others in as they are able to do so.

We said good-bye to him and his group with real affection in our hearts, particularly for him. He is a remarkable man, in my judgment. He appears to be entirely selfless in his attitude. I have felt a deep regret that we did not baptize him, although I am satisfied that he will be baptized within a matter of weeks and that it has been just as well that we make provisions to school him in the procedures of the Church before baptizing him. I had intended that President Quealy baptize him rather than that I do so and President Quealy was of the same opinion that we ought to wait until others could be baptized at the same time.[3]

I go to sleep somewhat troubled in my mind over not performing the ordinance in his behalf, but fully satisfied that good has been accomplished by our coming here and that the end results will be very much worthwhile and in harmony with the Lord's will. I would hope that a branch might be established here of people of what we might term the middle class and that as they become strong they can bring others into the Church, including the poor. This we have explained to Brother Paul. This marks the end of our visit to Coimbatore.

---

[3]Paul Thiruthuvodoss was baptized into the Church on February 7, 1965, by Jay A. Quealy, Jr.

X

SINGAPORE and INDONESIA

SINGAPORE and INDONESIA

The beginnings of missionary work in Singapore and Indonesia are of very recent date. The country of Singapore, comprising a population of about two million people, was dedicated for the preaching of the gospel on April 14, 1969, and the land of Indonesia on October 26, 1969, both by Elder Ezra Taft Benson of the Council of the Twelve. Since the minutes of these two dedicatory services comprise practically all significant history of the Church in these areas of Southeast Asia thus far, they are fully presented here.

The Dedication of Singapore

Elder and Sister Benson, in company with President W. Brent Hardy and Sister Hardy of the Southern Far East Mission, as well as forty-six other persons, including British, Americans, Malays, and Chinese, gathered at the site previously chosen for the dedication of Singapore, a hill known as Mount Faber.

The dedicatory services were conducted by President Hardy. Under the direction of Elder Rhett Todd Bake, those present sang "High on a Mountain Top," after which President Greg Gubler, the branch president, offered the opening prayer. President Hardy then spoke briefly, discussing the significance of the occasion and its importance to the furthering of the preaching of the gospel to the people of Asia. He traced briefly the history of the branch from a group under the direction of Roger Deeley, with less than ten members, to a branch with more than eighty participants. Brother Benson then offered the following remarks regarding the purpose of dedications by the Twelve:

My beloved brethren and sisters, this is a very historic and memorable occasion. I rejoice in the opportunity of meeting with you on this beautiful site overlooking this lovely nation and this beautiful city. It has been customary for many, many years for the Church to dedicate various nations for the preaching of the gospel. Sometimes the dedication takes place shortly after missionary work has started, as in the case here.

As I recall, the Prophet Joseph inaugurated these dedications in his day. When the Church went into new countries, it was not uncommon for him to authorize representatives of the Twelve to dedicate a particular land or country for the preaching of the gospel. Way back in 1841 he set apart Orson Hyde to go to the Holy Land. We haven't been preaching the gospel there yet, but the land was dedicated for the return of the Jews and for the preaching of the gospel, and eventually, of course, we will be preaching the gospel in that land.

A few months ago Sister Benson and I stood on a mountainside above the Piedmont Valley in northern Italy, as we dedicated that land, under the direction of President David O. McKay, for the preaching of the gospel. In 1946, I stood in the little nation of Finland and dedicated that land for the preaching of the gospel. And so as we dedicate a land, we more or less turn the key. We open the door for the beginning of organized proselyting, organized preaching of the gospel, that our Father's children in these particular lands may have an opportunity to hear the glad message of the gospel, which is for all of our Father's children, regardless of where they may be.

And so we come here on this occasion. And I come here authorized by President David O. McKay, whom we sustain as a prophet, seer, and a revelator, and President of the Church, to dedicate this land for the preaching of the gospel in organized fashion. And we expect confidently that thousands upon thousands of people in this choice country will hear the message and will accept the gospel, and that this may someday become a center from which the gospel can be directed and sent into other countries which have not yet heard the message of the restored gospel. So to me this is a very historic, a very momentous, and a very important occasion, and one that I am sure will lead to great achievements and the great spread of the gospel in this important part of the earth. Here we have millions upon hundreds of millions of people in these Asiatic countries that have not yet heard the gospel. This will be a training ground for missionaries and others who will be able to go out from here to carry the message to other nations in Asia.

Then Elder Benson offered a heartfelt prayer of dedication. He thanked the Lord for the spread of his work throughout the earth, and that the day of the gospel has come to Asia. He expressed gratitude for the spirit of freedom and love of liberty that is manifest among the people of Singapore. His prayer then included these inspiring words:

> May this nation be preserved in peace, and in freedom, that people may live here and enjoy an opportunity to carry on their chosen vocations in their respective fields without molestation and conflict with other nations. May this nation be preserved in peace and freedom, Father, in all the days to come.
>
> I turn the key, Holy Father, to open the door to the fullness of the gospel to be carried here among thy children. And Holy Father, wilt thou prosper the work. May the work in this part of thy vineyard move forward until it reaches the hearts of thousands upon thousands of thy children, all who are honest in heart. And may those who come here from other lands be touched also by the spirit of the gospel because of what will transpire here. Father, we feel to ask a further blessing upon this land, that in due course this nation may serve as a center from which the gospel may be directed to other lands that will be the means of spreading even beyond this nation the truths of the everlasting gospel and the building up of thy kingdom among thy children as they enjoy the saving principles of thy great plan of salvation.

The dedicatory services were closed with the singing of "We Thank Thee, O God, for a Prophet," after which Roger Deeley, the first group leader assigned in Singapore under the direction of the Southern Far East Mission, offered the closing prayer.

Following the dedicatory service, the group went to downtown Singapore and held a meeting at the MSA building. In attendance were eighty-nine members and investigators—Indians, Chinese, Malays, British, and Americans. The meeting was conducted by the branch president, Greg Gubler. Brother Eddy Chew offered the opening prayer, and Sister Cheung Lai Ching led the music. Two Singapore branch members were then called upon to bear their testimonies; Sister Cheung Lai Ching and Brother William Soh spoke of their introduction and conversion to the Church and of their thankfulness for the gospel. President Hardy then spoke briefly regarding the family, family home evening, and the importance and simplicity of the gospel. Sister Benson spoke on the joys of her own family life. Elder Benson, the concluding speaker, counseled on the importance of home and gave a message from President McKay: "Remember who you are and act accordingly."

The closing song was "Guide Us, O Thou Great Jehovah," and the closing prayer was offered by Sister Dora Ho. A good spirit was reported in all of these meetings.

The following morning Elder and Sister Benson and President Hardy left Singapore for Hong Kong. Theirs had been an inspirational and historic visit.

Elders Ezra Taft Benson (center) and Bruce R. McConkie, left, supervisors of the Oriental missions of the Church, discuss the boundaries of the new Southeast Asian Mission with G. Carlos Smith, the first president, prior to his departure for Singapore in October, 1969.

The Land of Indonesia

Dedicatory service, near Bagor, South of Djakarta,
Sunday, October 26, 1969

Conducted by President Bruce R. McConkie

President McConkie:

Our purpose this morning is to comply with the direction of the First Presidency and dedicate the Indonesian land and nations, the islands, and the people, and all things that appertain to this, to the preaching of the gospel. And I think I might say that when we perform a dedication in the Church, what we actually do is dedicate the people and the resources of the Church. When you dedicate a building for worship, in effect what you do is dedicate the people to the cause of righteousness, so that when they say "Amen" to the dedicatory prayer, they are covenanting to use the house of worship that has been given to the Lord to further his interests and his program.

For all practical purposes, when we dedicate the Indonesian lands to the preaching of the gospel, we're both opening the door to the spread of truth in the nation involved and dedicating the resources of the Church and the talents and abilities of the members of the Church to spread the gospel in that nation. We have a commission from the Lord that has come by latter-day revelation, a direct command that we're to take the gospel that was restored through the instrumentality primarily of Joseph Smith to every nation and kindred and tongue and people. The Lord has decreed that the name of Joseph Smith will be known for good and evil among all people, and that in every nation and among every kindred the voice of truth and the voice of testimony will be heard before the second coming of the Son of Man. He has also decreed that before that day comes, out of every nation will be assembled people who will come into the Church and kingdom and be inheritors of the fullness of its blessings.

One of the revelations says that when the Lord comes there will be those out of every nation and kindred and tongue and people who will reign with him on earth for a thousand years as kings and priests. What this means is that we're not only going to preach the gospel in all nations before the Second Coming, but we're going to have success in all nations. People will come out of the darkness of the past into the light of revealed latter-day truth; they'll join the Church; and they'll become inheritors of the fullness of the blessings of the gospel.

Just as rapidly as the strength and ability of the Church permits, just as rapidly as we are big enough and large enough and strong enough to go into an added part of the Lord's vineyard, this is what we do. This is what is transpiring here on this occasion. We're opening the door. We're going into a new part of the Lord's vineyard to take the most important message there is in the world. There isn't anything in the world as important as the gospel of Jesus Christ. Out of it come peace for us here and eternal reward in the mansions, the realms, that are to be.

Brother Benson referred to a passage of scripture in the first section of the Doctrine and Covenants that is part of one of the decrees under which we work. The Lord has said that "the voice of warning should be unto all people by the mouths of my disciples whom I have chosen in these last days." And then he issued the promise and the assurance, "And they shall go forth, and none shall stay them, for I the Lord have commanded them." Well, we'll have problems to solve and difficulties will arise, but through it all the work will advance and progress and grow and increase, here and elsewhere and everywhere, until finally the knowledge of God covers the earth as the waters cover the sea. It's the Lord's work, and there is an eternal, invarying, absolute principle that truth will prevail. And since we have the truth, the ultimate end of this work is to prevail and to triumph and to grow over all things. . . .

In the one hundred and twelfth section of the Doctrine and Covenants we have the instruction given to the Council of the Twelve to open the door to the preaching of the gospel in all nations. We have the instruction that where they cannot be personally, they are to call agents and representatives and send them by their united voice; so what Brother Benson will do in this dedicatory prayer is turn the key on behalf of the Indonesian people. He will open the door and the way will then be available for the expansion and the growth of the work here. And the operation of the work will be in the hands of President G. Carlos Smith, who has been given the keys of the presidency of the Southeast Asia Mission. As the representative of the Twelve, having been sent by their united voice, he will direct the affairs of the ministry and the laborers in the building up of the kingdom here.

Without any question, the Lord will bless and prosper the

cause that is involved. Souls will be brought to Christ. There will be people saved in great numbers in the celestial kingdom of heaven who otherwise would not have had that inheritance had it not been for the ministry that has somewhat begun, but is now to begin anew on an expanded and enlarged basis.

It's a great privilege for all of us to be here on this occasion. The work is true. It is God's work. His hand is in it. The Lord is directing the destiny and affairs of his kingdom. I have a testimony of the divinity of the work and know that Jesus is the Lord and Joseph Smith is his prophet, that Joseph Smith is the revelator of the knowledge of Christ and the knowledge of salvation for this day, and further that the Church as now constituted and operated is going forward under the Lord's direction. And I pray, as was prayed in the opening prayer, that the work will grow and prosper here as the Lord's providences indicate, in the name of Jesus Christ. Amen.

Now, Brother Brent Hardy, the president of the Southern Far East Mission, and to be the president of the Hong Kong-Taiwan Mission effective November 1 when the division occurs, will speak to us and will give us his views and feelings relative to the glorious work we are undertaking now.

President W. Brent Hardy:

Brothers and sisters, I would like this morning to have my words reflect primarily my testimony and my gratitude to the Lord for this day. This is the second time this year that Brother Benson and I and our brothers and sisters have participated in the dedication of a great land.

As I read the scriptures, study the prophecies, ponder the utterances of our Father in heaven through his prophets, I am daily grateful for the opportunity that I have and we have, as brothers and sisters in the Church, of participating in the fulfilling of those prophecies. We read in the Old Testament of the prophecy of Daniel, in which he talks about a stone being cut out without hands and rolling forth to fill the entire earth. That is part of what is going on here today. And I hope you young people who are here today, in years to come, will not forget this sight you see today and what you are being told, because you too, by your inheritance, by your parentage, have a great part to play in the growth of the Church in these latter days. And your being here puts you in a position to participate in many ways, in great ways, in the growth of the gospel. But you, and all of us, we must keep the commandments and stay close to the faith, because days will not be easy.

The work here in Indonesia will not be easy, but it will succeed because it is the work of God. As we rode up this morning I looked at the many hundreds and thousands of people that we passed by going about their daily work, selling bananas, pineapples, taking tickets on buses, driving their ox carts, their little horse carts, washing their clothes, unaware of what was taking place in their great country on the twenty-sixth of October, 1969. They have had many great things happen in their country, many heart-breaking things, many momentous things, many historical things. But the event that you and I, the few of us here today, are participating in is the greatest thing that has happened to Indonesia, and yet so few, this few here, know about it. But that won't always be the case. The message, the responsibility, is now to see that every man and woman and child knows why we're here, that we're here because the Lord has commanded us to be here, and that what we bring to them through peace, through the message and the blessings of the gospel, is that thing that they have sought for so many years.

I am grateful to my Father in heaven for the opportunity I have had to participate thus far in the growth of the gospel in Indonesia. I'm grateful to see that the work is now being fully instituted, and the land is being dedicated to the preaching of the message of the resurrection and the divinity of Christ and the principles of the everlasting gospel. I bear you my testimony that this work is true. Though men may be weak, the gospel stays true, and only we ourselves can prevent us from receiving the blessings of the gospel. The only way we can prevent the Lord from blessing us is through disobedience. That's an eternal principle.

I bear you my testimony and add my witness that this man who stands here today is indeed a representative of the

Lord upon this earth; he is indeed a servant of the Lord sent here by the direction of the prophet, seer, and revelator for the Church, President David O. McKay, and acts as a mouthpiece for the Lord Jesus Christ in doing this work here today. I add to yours my testimony and bear you my witness in the name of Jesus Christ. Amen.

President G. Carlos Smith:

My mind is at ease and my soul is peaceful. I'm grateful to the Lord that I have his assurance that what is being done here today is his will. I've had a great deal of anxiety about coming out in this part of the world, and all of my fears have been alleviated since coming here. I am sort of a rebellious spirit, and I like to take shortcuts. Many times I take shortcuts when the results are the long way around. I wondered why Brother Benson wanted to come out two hours from town, why we just couldn't take care of this work in the park in town or some other place. And now I see why, Brother Benson.

I want to say to these young people that we're engaged in the Lord's work. This isn't man's work. The Lord has appointed his servants to direct his affairs in the world. And Brother Benson is one of these men whom the Lord has called and instructed and sent forth to be a special ambassador to all the world wherever he is so directed by the First Presidency and the Twelve. Brother Benson has seen fit to come here at this spot at this time, and this is the will of the Lord. I want you young people to remember it all of your lives. You're standing on a hallowed spot of ground, and that good feeling that you feel is the Spirit of the Lord. He's mindful of us. He knows we are here, and he is pleased. I'm grateful to be a part of this new movement in this part of the world, new to these people but old to the Lord, of course.

I am grateful for the Prophet Joseph Smith. And I want to witness to you that I know in very deed that he is a prophet of God, and I hope and pray that someday I'll be worthy to stand before that man and receive his approbation and his love. I love the Lord with all my heart. I love our Heavenly Father, and I'm so grateful to him for what he's done for me.

I bear my witness: this is God's work; he lives; his Son, Jesus the Christ, lives, and he stands at the head of this church, for this is the Church of Jesus Christ—not man's church, but the Lord's Church, that we must be about his business. I pray that his Spirit will attend each of us, that those who live here in this country will have the spirit of missionary work, that we will long to bear our witness to our neighbors and our friends, and that by our actions the people that we associate with will see our good works and glorify our Father who is in heaven. And I know this, as I stand here with you—if we fail to do this we will be held accountable, and it will be a sorrowful day when we report our ministry. I say these things to you, expressing my love and appreciation and my gratitude for each one, my gratitude for my testimony, and I do so in the name of the Lord Jesus Christ. Amen.

President Bruce R. McConkie:

These are two great men. They represent the Lord. They are on his errand. The work prospers under their direction. We would like now to ask Sister Hardy to sing for us "As the Dew From Heaven Distilling."

Sister Hardy Sings:

As the dew from heaven distilling
Gently on the grass descends
And revives it, thus fulfilling
What thy providence intends.

Let thy doctrine, Lord, so gracious,
Thus descending from above,
Blest by thee, prove efficacious
To fulfil thy work of love.

Lord, behold this congregation;
Precious promises fulfil;
From thy holy habitation
Let the dews of life distil.

Let our cry come up before thee;
Thy sweet Spirit shed around,

So the people shall adore thee
And confess the joyful sound.

President McConkie:

We will sing "We Thank Thee, O God, for a Prophet."
Then we will hear from Brother Benson, who will also offer
the dedicatory prayer. After this we'll invite Brother Peter
Grimm, whose influence past and present has been great and
majestic for the benefit of the Church in much of Asia, and
whose influence will continue to radiate for the good of the
cause, to offer a word of benediction.

Elder Benson:

I rejoice with you, my beloved brothers and sisters, on
this very historic and memorable occasion. I have enjoyed so
much the words of my brethren, the lovely singing by the
group, and this beautiful solo by Sister Hardy. My heart is
full of gratitude to the Lord for this sacred occasion.

This is the fourth time that I remember that I've been
privileged to represent our beloved leader, President David O.
McKay, the First Presidency, and the Twelve, in dedicating a
land for the preaching of the gospel. In 1946, right after
the war, I stood in a grove of trees on a big flat rock on a
little mound way up in northern Finland as we dedicated that
land. Later, in 1965, we stood on the mountainside overlooking the beautiful Piedmont Valley as we dedicated the land
of Italy for the work in that country. In both of these countries
I have seen the work flourish and grow. I have seen the Spirit
operating on the people, both members and nonmembers alike.
I have seen the hand of the Lord in evidence. As Brother
Hardy has mentioned, just a few months ago we stood on a
prominent rising overlooking the city of Singapore as we
dedicated that land for sacred purposes. And now we stand
here on this lovely prominence overlooking this beautiful
countryside, the mountains and the hills, and the rice fields
in the distance, as we proceed to dedicate this choice land.

I think that never before have I felt so completely sure
that we're opening the door to a very fruitful field. I have

already come to love these people as I've watched them, as I've talked with them, and I've learned a little more about them. And I have every confidence that the Lord will bless us and those who come here, and that there will be a rich harvest come from this great country. The Church will prosper, branches will be raised up, districts will be organized, and I'm sure someday a great mission of the Church will center in these islands alone. These are good people, and I'm sure the Lord loves them and wants them to have the truth.

Now we're opening the door so that missionaries may come in and so that the truth may be spread and the knowledge of God and his great purposes in these latter days can be revealed to them. As Sister Hardy started singing, I turned to that wonderful hymn by Parley P. Pratt. I think I have never attended a dedication but what I think of some of the words in the hymn "The Morning Breaks; The Shadows Flee." He said,

> The morning breaks; the shadows flee;
> Lo, Zion's standard is unfurled.
> The dawning of a brighter day
> Majestic rises on the world.
>
> The clouds of error disappear
> Before the rays of truth divine;
> The glory bursting from afar
> Wide o'er the nation soon will shine.
>
> Jehovah speaks! Let earth give ear,
> And Gentile nations turn and live.
> His mighty arm is making bare,
> His covenant people to receive.

And so this message that we bear to the world is a world message. Surely an event as significant as the coming of the Lord Jesus Christ and of God the Father is an event that should challenge the interest of all of our Father's children. The greatest event that has transpired in this world since the resurrection of the Master occurred in that Sacred Grove in 1820 when these two Heavenly Personages came and appeared to the boy prophet in answer to humble prayer. That was the opening of the last and the greatest of all gospel dispensations in preparation for the spread of the gospel throughout the nations of the world. There is no power on earth or in hell that can stop this work. It will roll forth, and our Father's children will be given an opportunity to hear the truth of the message.

As Brother McConkie has quoted from the Doctrine and Covenants, the introduction to the Lord's Book of Commandments in these latter days, he said, "Hearken, O ye people of my Church, saith the voice of him who dwells on high, . . . yea, . . . Hearken ye people from afar; and ye that are upon the islands of the sea, listen together." I've thought of that time and time again since we came here. "Ye that are upon the islands of the sea, listen together." There's no nation in the world that has more islands than this nation, and I am sure that they are going to listen together because, as the revelation continues, ". . . the voice of the Lord is unto all men, and there is none to escape."

And so this voice of the Lord, the restored gospel of Jesus Christ, the same principles, must go to the wonderful people on these islands. I'm grateful to have a small part in it, as I know each one of you is; and I expect with great confidence and assurance that the work will grow and prosper here in these islands among this good people, that the Lord will raise up good friends for the Church. He's already demonstrated that in a most remarkable manner. He'll raise up further friends for the Church among high officials of government, men of influence, as well as among the humble and sweet characters of these islands. So I have no fear but what the gospel will prosper and the work of the Lord will grow and increase in this wonderful nation.

I express gratitude to the Lord on behalf of all of you for the manner in which the way has been made open that we could come here today and on this lovely spot utter a prayer of gratitude and dedication and thanksgiving to the Lord for the rich blessings that we have seen with our own eyes and experience in our hearts and that we know will continue as the work rolls forth among this good people.

May God bless us, my brethren and sisters, that we will ever remember this day. I hope that we might consider coming here annually, the Saints in the area not too far removed from here. That's done in some countries. I remember going with the people of Czechoslovakia up on the mountain where Brother John A. Widtsoe stood and dedicated that land. They go each year. We, of course, don't worship spots of ground, but this spot has been made sacred because of this event here today, as it has in Finland, Italy, and many other places, and in South America, where Brother Ballard went. And so it would be a lovely thing if maybe once a year there could be a group come here and have a little service and thank the Lord again for opening the door to this great nation of 130 million people. God bless us and help us to appreciate the blessings we enjoy and to live worthy of them I pray in the name of Jesus Christ. Amen.

And now if you'll unite your faith and prayers, we will proceed with the dedicatory prayer.

Dedicatory Prayer

O God, our Heavenly, all wise and Eternal Father, in humility and gratitude we approach thy holy throne in the attitude of prayer through the name of thy Beloved Son, our Savior and Redeemer.

As thou seest, Holy Father, we are assembled here as a small body of thy devoted Saints, members of thy great church and kingdom, with gratitude and thanksgiving in our hearts, overlooking this beautiful valley and the hills and mountains, the handiwork of thy hands, Holy Father.

We rejoice in this opportunity. We pray that thou will forgive us of any of our imperfections and sins and not withhold from us thy Spirit as we pray unto thee on this thy holy day.

Father in heaven, we express our gratitude that thou did see fit to come with thy beloved Son and appear to the boy prophet and thereby usher in a new dispensation of the gospel of thy beloved Son. We thank thee, Holy Father, that thou has seen fit to send heavenly messengers, bearing important keys, messengers bearing the priesthood of God, as a means of opening this great gospel dispensation and retoring the fullness of the saving principles which are so important to thy children and so much needed in the world.

We thank thee for the program of thy church, for the growth of thy church throughout the world. We thank thee, Father in heaven, for the great organizations, auxiliaries, and priesthood organizations that are part of thy great church and kingdom. We realize the richness of the program, Heavenly Father. We have felt it in our own lives; we have seen it in the lives of our children, and we are so grateful that the time has come when the gospel might penetrate this great land, that the people of this land may be privileged to enjoy the fruits of the gospel and the rich program of thy great church and kingdom.

And so this day, Holy Father, under authority from our beloved leader, thy mouthpiece and prophet here on the earth, President David O. McKay, the First Presidency, and the Council of the Twelve, we dedicate this land, Holy Father, and all that pertains to it. The land itself, the physical properties, the good people who live here, and every part and segment of this good land, we dedicate unto thee for thy great work, for the accomplishment of thy purposes, for the spread of thy great gospel. And, O Father, we dedicate this land under the authority of the Holy Priesthood of God invested in thy humble servant and shared by others who are here, and in the authority and power of the holy apostleship, Father, I dedicate this land for sacred purposes, for the spread of thy work, for the upbuilding of thy cause, and for the blessing of thy people, thy children here.

Father, millions of them are in darkness. We bless them that the scales of darkness may drop from their eyes, that they may have vision and the spirit of discernment and may be able to see clearly, when the gospel is presented to them, the step that they should take.

Father in heaven, bless these humble people, many of them living almost in abject poverty. May the gospel reach them. May thy servants come here in great numbers and carry this message to these thy children, that they may be lifted up, that their vision may be raised, that they may get a picture of the purposes of life and its meaning and the great hope they may have for the future.

Father in heaven, open the way. Touch the hearts of the leaders of this great nation. We are grateful for their kindness. We pray thee that thou will reward them for the help which they have already rendered. And will thou touch their hearts, Father, that they too may receive a witness of the divinity of thy great work. Bless them in their leadership.

This great nation has come through a very critical and crucial period, Father. They are lovers of freedom. And thou knowest, Holy Father, that the gospel can only prosper in an atmosphere of freedom. Thou knowest the insidious influences that are at work here in the earth, counterfeits to the gospel, that would destroy thy work. Thou knowest, Holy Father, that the fight we have now is but a continuation of the war in heaven. Will thou, Holy Father, hedge up the way of the adversary in this great country, that the great Godless Communist conspiracy may have no influence here, that people may not have to further shed their blood in order to oppose this great evil.

Let the love of the holy gospel spread throughout this land. May they receive a wintess of the divine mission of thy beloved Son and the ministry of the Prophet Joseph. May they know thee, Holy Father. They love thee although they do not understand the nature of thy divine personality. But, O Father, may they know, may they receive a testimony that thou art their Father and that thy beloved Son, Jesus the Christ, is their Savior and Redeemer.

And may they know that prophets have guided this work from Joseph Smith to the present day, that the inspiration of heaven is directing this work.

May they come to love the President of the Church, the General Authorities, those who bear the priesthood of God who labor among them, their mission president, branch presidents, missionaries, and all who serve. And may they be able to see, Holy Father, the beauties and the glories and the blessings of the everlasting gospel.

May they arise and shine forth as a nation. Wilt thou prosper them, Heavenly Father. Bless their land that it may be productive. Wilt thou impede the movement of pests and disease among their crops that is taking such a toll at the present time. May they be blessed with scientific knowledge and inspiration sufficient that they might be more effective in their productive enterprises, that the people may have a higher standard of living, that industries may be established here that will provide employment and will provide income for these good people.

And, O Father, bless them as they receive the gospel that they may have a desire to pay their honest tithes, to maintain the standards of thy church, to live the gospel fully.

We thank thee for this choice land, for these good people. We feel in our hearts, Holy Father, that they are humble in spirit, that they are industrious, that they have a spirit of integrity and honesty and honor which is most commendable and which in large measure, Heavenly Father, will make it easier for them to see and to accept the gospel.

We have already come to love them, and we pray that the missionaries who come here may love them as they labor among them, that they may develop a great spirit of brotherhood and fellowship between the missionaries and among the Saints as this great work prospers and grows.

Bless thy servant who will have responsibility as the president of the South[east] Asia Mission, that he may enjoy thy inspiration, that he may see clearly his duty, that friends may be raised up for his need, that he may give direction to the growth and the development of the work here in these islands, that the work may prosper.

We have the assurance, Holy Father, through thy Spirit, that the work will prosper; thousands upon thousands, yea, hundreds of thousands of these good people will be brought to a knowledge of the truth through thy blessings and through the efforts of thy servants. For this assurance we express our gratitude and thanksgiving unto thee.

And now, Holy Father, we do not wish to multiply words before thee. We love thee and thy great work. We love our Savior and Redeemer, thy beloved Son. We love thy prophet and mouthpiece here on the earth, President David O. McKay, thine aged servant. Wilt thou bless him, Holy Father. Give him the energy and strength he needs so long as thou seest fit to have him remain with us. Bless all associated with him.

And bless all who serve the great missionary cause particularly, the mission presidents and thus the members, with the spirit of missionary work, that they may heed the counsel of the prophet and every member be a missionary, that they may give referrals to the missionaries, that they may invite people into their homes and into their meetings, that there may be a rapid spread of thy work in this part of thy vineyard.

O Father, we thank thee for all that we have and all that we are and all that we enjoy at thy hands.

We are grateful for our personal testimonies of the divinity of thy great work, for membership in thy church, for the blessings of the priesthood in our home, for the eternity of the marriage covenant, for our families, and all that makes life, for the blessings of the gospel so enjoyable and so comforting and so reassuring.

And so as we come to the end of this little service, Holy Father, we rededicate our lives unto thee and all that we have and are to the upbuilding of thy work in the earth and the furtherance of truth and righteousness in the world and we do it all in the name of thy beloved Son, our Savior and Redeemer, even Jesus the Christ. Amen.

XI

Language and translation

Language
and translation

The devil must have invented the Chinese language to keep the missionaries out of China.

John Fryer[1]

The Translation Services Department in Asia was officially organized in March, 1968, with Kan Watanabe as manager, Yasuhiro Matsushita as coordinator for the Japanese area, Han In Sang as coordinator for the Korean area, and Ng Kat Hing as coordinator for the Chinese area. Supervising the department were Bishop Victor L. Brown, counselor in the Presiding Bishopric; J. Thomas Fyans, general Church supervisor of translation; and D'Monte W. Coombs, supervisor of Far East translation. Later John E. Carr was assigned as the general church supervisor.

The work has been progressing at a rapid pace. As of January, 1970, the Chinese and Korean areas had each translated about 6,000 pages of Church literature and the Japanese area had translated about 9,000 pages, including all of the priesthood and auxiliary manuals. All programs of the Church are fully available in Japan, and almost all are now available to the Chinese and Koreans.

The Asian area Translation Services Department has great challenges and opportunities ahead as new missions open in areas of the Far East where Church literature is not yet available in the native languages. But there has already been a significant start.

---

[1]A nineteenth century Protestant missionary in China who later founded the Department of Oriental Languages at the University of California at Berkeley.

Kan Watanabe, manager, Translation Services Department (appointed president of the Japan West Mission in March, 1970).

Ng Kat Hing, Chinese area

Hang In Sang, Korean Area

Yasuhiro Matsushita, Japanese Area

Translation Services in Asia

Japanese Book of Mormon

On January 11, 1904, Horace S. Ensign, second president of the Japan Mission, in a meeting of all his missionaries in Tokyo, announced that the time had arrived to begin work on the translation of the Book of Mormon into the Japanese language. According to Alma O. Taylor's account, President Ensign called upon the elders "to devote their spare moments to this labor, translating any part of the book they desired, and instructed them to preserve their translations. These translations, he stated, could be gathered together later and be compared, revised and finally made into a complete translation of the whole."

None of the missionaries responded as wholeheartedly to this request of the president as did Elder Taylor. On Monday night, January 18, he later reported, "Being alone in a little six mat room in the rear part of the Makinoya Hotel, as I sat crosslegged upon a zabuton on the grass-mat floor, with a low native table before me, I made my first effort at the translation of the Book of Mormon. I began at the first of the title page, believing that to start at the very beginning was the proper course." Elder Taylor's diligence was soon recognized by President Ensign, who assigned the entire labor of translation to him. He was set apart to that work on July 17, 1904.

Alma Taylor succeeded Horace Ensign as Japan Mission president on July 4, 1905. Since the demands of this new assignment frequently took him away from his translation studies for prolonged periods of time, he called upon others to help, particularly Elder Fred A. Caine. President Taylor had been in the mission field a little less than three years when the translation project was entrusted to him. It took one year and nine months before his first draft was finished, on March 21, 1906. His confidence and skill in the language had increased tremendously as the result of long months of translation experience. Recognizing this and that the merits of the first part of the translation were therefore "fewer and inferior" to those of the later parts, he determined to make a revision of the entire manuscript. This thorough-going revision started on May 14, 1906, and was concluded December 6, 1907. President Taylor's informants and scribes included Yasubeie Chiba, Hachiro Mori (who was baptized while engaged in helping on this revision), and Takeshiro Sakuraba.

President Taylor's written translation had followed the so-called *gembunitchi* style of language, something approaching colloquial Japanese. Upon sending copies of the translation of First Nephi to two reputable Japanese critics, he was informed that the *busho,* or literary language, would have been much better, as it would have lent greater power and dignity to the book. Many consultations and much prayer on the subject finally resulted in a decision to change to the *busho* style. Since Alma Taylor felt unqualified to produce a highly literary translation of the Book of Mormon, he selected Hirogoro Hirai of Waseda University to do the work. An agreement was entered into on September 2, 1907, but owing to unsavory reports in a Japanese newspaper regarding Mr. Hirai's character and his continuing connections with Waseda University (in violation of the articles of the agreement), Mr. Hirai was dismissed. On July 29, 1908, after consultation with Jujiro Tsubouchi, a famous writer and head of the department of literature at Waseda, and Kinnosuke Natsume, a national literary figure, Mr. Hirocharu Ikuta, a graduate of the Imperial University in Tokyo and author of several books, was employed to finish the translation. By July 24, 1908, the final corrections of the Book of Mormon manuscript were made, the eighth anniversary of the day Alma O. Taylor had left home on his mission to Japan.

It was decided that the first edition of the Book of Mormon in Japanese should consist of 5,000 copies, bound in good cloth. The Shueisha Daiichi Koba firm was selected as printers because their bid was the lowest offered. On October 6, 1909, the proofreading was finished. On October 6, two bound copies were rushed out for filing with the Home Department of the Japanese government. Specially bound copies in "deep cardinal red and deep violet morocco" with a cover design in gold and silver were sent to the Emperor and Empress. The copy for the Crown Prince was the same design in black morocco. Copies were also prepared for the Empress and Crown Princess in pure white morocco. Regular morocco copies were prepared for the heads of the various departments of government. Translated into Japanese, the body of the Book of Mormon filled 942 pages, many more than the English editions. The translation of the English title page filled both sides of one sheet.

Elder Taylor has summarized the monumental effort to translate and publish the first copies of the Book of Mormon into the Japanese language in this way:

> It was just five years and nine months from the day of the first appointment to the day of delivery of the first 1,000 completed copies. The time from the day I was entrusted with the entire work to the day the translation proper was completed was four years, ten months and twenty-four days. The printing, proofreading and binding of the first edition, excluding the 80 copies in special binding, covered a period of eight months and twenty-five days. The number of critics of my work is five—Elder Caine and four natives. The number of scribes who labored on the translation is eight—Elder Caine and seven natives. In making the translation and reviews, I read the English text verse by verse five times and after writing the Romanji manuscript with my own hand, I read the translation twice in Romanji and seven times after it was copied in the ideographs. It has been read seven times by the critics. None of these include proof readings. Four manuscripts, one in Romanji and three in the native characters, have been required.
>
> The Romanji manuscript consisted of twenty-one hundred pages. The first character manuscript filled fourteen volumes and covered 2,400 pages. The second character manuscript required 27 volumes and filled 3,600 pages, while the last or printer's manuscript filled 34 volumes and over 5,000 pages. The reason for the increase in pages in the character manuscripts is that each time wider spaces were left between the lines. The last two manuscripts were preserved intact. All but samples of the first two were destroyed as valueless, even as relics. There are in the translation without counting references, tables of contents, tables of explanations, and testimonies, about 467,000 characters (not all different by any means). The fee for critics and scribes and incidental expense connected with the translation alone required a cash outlay of Yen 2,177.26. The printing and publication of the first edition, including special volumes for the Imperial Family, represents a cash outlay of Yen 2,614.97. Yen 1,588.89 was spent in advertising the edition. The book is retailed at one yen each, a liberal discount being allowed to all book stores.[2]

[2]From Alma O. Taylor's personal account. See Murray Nichols, *op. cit.*, Appendix B, for the complete report.

Japanese Translations After 1949

Tatsui Sato, after having been set apart as the official translator of the Japan Mission by Elder Matthew Cowley on June 12, 1949, was assigned by President Edward L. Clissold to translate the standard works of the Church into Japanese, starting with the Book of Mormon. It was felt that copies of the first edition of the Book of Mormon that were still available would have to be updated to keep abreast of the great changes in the Japanese language that took place between 1909 and 1949. Brother Sato worked simultaneously on all three of the restoration scriptures—the Book of Mormon, Doctrine and Covenants, and the Pearl of Great Price—over a period of nine years. The Book of Mormon was republished on May 30, 1957. The books were printed in attractive but inexpensive covers for 300 Yen ($0.84) for each of the three books of scripture. A leather-bound triple combination was printed at the same time and sold for 1,100 Yen ($3.07).

Chinese Book of Mormon

On January 29, 1966, a long-awaited event was announced in the *Church News*. The Book of Mormon had been printed in the Chinese script, in the written language of 700 million people.[3] The first copy was presented to President David O. McKay by Elder Gordon B. Hinckley of the Council of the Twelve, supervisor of Oriental missions of the Church. An inscription in the book read:

> This copy of the first edition of the Book of Mormon in Chinese was presented to David O. McKay, who 45 years ago, on January 9, 1921, accompanied by Elder Hugh J. Cannon, in the 'Forbidden City' of Peking dedicated and consecrated and set apart 'the Chinese realm for the preaching of the Gospel of Jesus Christ as restored in this dispensation through the Prophet Joseph Smith.'

> The Book of Mormon is now available in the language which is the mother tongue of more people than any other on earth.

---

[3]For a very interesting examination of translation problems, with suggested possible solutions as they relate to the Book of Mormon, see Robert J. Morris, "Some Problems of Translating Mormon Thought Into Chinese," *BYU Studies* (Winter, 1970), pp. 173-85.

May it go forth among them as a witness of the Son of God, the Savior of the World.

With sincere respect and deep affection.

Gordon B. Hinckley

President McKay responded to the presentation, saying, "This is a great event in the history of the Chinese people."

President David O. McKay receives a copy of the first edition of the Book of Mormon in Chinese from Elder Gordon B. Hinckley, January 29, 1966.

Several years prior to its publication, work on the Chinese translation was begun under the direction of President H. Grant Heaton and continued under the supervision of Robert S. Taylor. Under the presidency of Jay A. Quealy, Jr., two men were called and set apart by Elder Hinckley to bring the work to fruition: President Hu Wei-I, counselor to the mission president in the Taiwan Zone, who was born and educated on mainland China, and Elder Larry K. Browning, who had served a mission in Hong Kong and then went back to Taiwan under an educational grant from the University of California.

The Chinese Book of Mormon was printed in Hong Kong under the direction of President Keith M. Garner of the Southern Far East Mission. The first edition included a total of 5,000 copies.

The Doctrine and Covenants and Pearl of Great Price had not been published in the Chinese language as of January, 1970.

Korean Book of Mormon

It was an impressive list of "firsts" for President and Sister Rhee Ho Nam of Korea when they made their first trip to Salt Lake City to attend general conference in April, 1967.[4] They were the first Korean couple living in that mission to be sealed as husband and wife in a temple of the Lord. President Rhee was second counselor to the mission president.

The Rhees brought the first copies of the Book of Mormon printed in the Korean language for presentation to President McKay and to Elder Hinckley.

Although many attempts to complete a translation and publication of the Book of Mormon had been made by members and missionaries in Korea, including many weeks of concentrated effort by Kim Ho Jik, Hong Byong Sik, Chong T'ae Pan, Lynn Waddel, Bruce K. Grant, and Ronald K. Nielson, the work that culminated in the publication of that volume of

---

[4]The Rhees' eventful and inspirational visit to the United States is covered in detail in John D. Chase, "A Delightful Experience," *The White Field,* May, 1967, pp. 25-32.

scripture started in April of 1965. It began with Han In Sang, a Korean and full-time missionary who was assigned by President Gail E. Carr to complete a translation of the book. For that purpose Elder Han secluded himself in a study room of the Pusan Tong Ku Branch, drawing upon the work of his predecessors but in the main producing a work that bore the stamp of his own inspiration and skill. Elder Han's account of "My Part in Translating the Most Perfect Book Ever Written" is as follows:

"I never thought even in my dreams that I would be called on a mission or to become a translator of the Book of Mormon. I still feel some kind of uneasiness about my mission. It is not because I was a bad missionary or a trouble missionary or something like that. The reason is that I could not support my own mission with my *own money*. And in addition to that thought, I was the second local missionary to be called; Young B. Lee was the first, but I was the first one who was called to serve a full two years, and I had to work with about forty foreign missionaries as an unofficial representative of the Korean Saints. I had many difficulties: the difficulty of language, way of life, way of thinking, way of handling the problems, and more than those, I had just been released from Korean Marine Corps service.

"I accepted the assignment to translate the Book of Mormon with a determination that I would offer everything that I had for making it possible. I asked my Heavenly Father to help me in my work. I was very sick at the time with hepatitis and could not digest any food. But I knew that I would not die until I finished the translation completely. Elders Edwin Jensen, Tingey, Scoville, and Nielson were there at Pusan Tong Ku with me at that time. I used to work in the small room in the second floor of Pusan Tong Ku and the elders named my little room 'The Cage.'

"I tasted the real meaning of joy while I was working down there. I used to take the translation down to the elders and read for them and asked their advice and opinion. I still remember Elder Scoville because he was so eager to see the translation completed before his mission finished. Those missionaries helped me a great deal. They taught me things and passages that I could not understand clearly. I'm also grateful for President Carr and his help and for Elders Nielson and Burke and their help. I was very nervous while I was working on the translation. I was easily hurt by almost everything too.

"Many times when I had trouble in my heart I could not translate even one single verse, or one word. It sounded very strange even to my ears today but that is the way it was; I could not translate. Whenever I made mistakes, somehow my feelings used to go down deep and I felt a heavy weight that oppressed me. Then I would stop my work and check the translated pages and would find not once, not twice, but many times the mistakes.

"President Carr finished his mission before I was able to finish the work. I finished the translation on August 28, 1965. I reported to the new mission president, Spencer J. Palmer. Then I left for Marine summer camp. I felt freedom. I was free from pressure, work, and worry.

"When I returned from camp President Palmer asked me to prepare for the printing of the Book of Mormon. Frankly speaking I did not want to stay at the mission home and do anything more on the Book of Mormon. Now I'm grateful to President Palmer for his love and his concern. He really helped me so that I could carry on my mission.

"I started the proofreading with Sister Park Kee Ok. Brother Bruce Grant, who was in Korea in the military service and attending to university work as well, worked on the arrangement of the index and footnotes. He was an expert on the Book of Mormon project. He arranged all the names in the Book of Mormon and made a list for pronouncing words.

"Brother Ji Yong Dal helped by doing some work on the index and in correcting technical errors. It was very hard to arrange the footnotes because of the difference in the sentence order of the English and Korean languages. We had to check sentence by sentence and page by page.

"One day President Palmer and I read a newspaper which

explained that the Korean government would eliminate Chinese characters from all public printings. We cut this out and sent it to Elder Hinckley, and with his advice, decided not to use any Chinese characters in the Korean Book of Mormon. It would contain only the native *han'gul* phonetic script. President Palmer decided to print it in modern style, that is, you open the book from the left like in western books, and the sentences go from left to right, horizontally. This is the style of publication now commonly used in the Korean publishing world.

"Quite often people ask me how I translated the phrase 'It came to pass' into Korean. I didn't translate it literally, but only included the meaning in every phrase. There is no proper word for this in the Korean dictionary or Korean language. But this is only an example.

"Again I would like to thank President Palmer. He was his brother's keeper. When I needed help, President Palmer was there with ample nourishment of various kinds. When I felt sorrow, sadness, and weariness, he always brought comfort and peace. I caused problems purposely many times because I loved him and respected him too much. He watched over me so closely that I could not fail while I was working on the Book of Mormon.

"The people of Samhwa Printing Company had been waiting for a completed translation of the Book of Mormon for a long time. They were even more eager than the Korean Saints. Of course it meant business for them. They hurried the typesetting and transcribing and making the negatives. The paper had been purchased by President Carr years before and had been sleeping in the printer's storeroom. We had a lot of trouble getting it because the receipt for it had been lost. Then another serious problem arose. Samhwa reported that he could not print with that paper, not because of its quality but because of the condition it was in. It wouldn't go through the press without wrinkling. Finally, we were able to make arrangements with Pojinjae Publishers in another part of town to handle the job because they had a special press that could do it.

"In closing, I would like to bear my testimony. I know the Church is true and the Book of Mormon is true, no matter what people may say. Even if the Lord should reject my translation, I will still depend upon him in all things. In the name of our Savior. *In Sang Han.*"

A total of 2,000 economy issues and 500 gilt-edged black Morocco bound copies of the Book of Mormon were printed. Special issues in white leather were sent to President McKay, Elder Hinckley, and Elder Marion D. Hanks, other General Authorities who have visited Korea, and to President Palmer, Elder Han, and others in Korea who had assisted in the work. Copies were also presented to leaders in the Korean church and civic community.

The Doctrine and Covenants and Pearl of Great Price in Korean

In March, 1966, Brother Chong T'ae Pan was called and set apart by President Spencer Palmer to be responsible for the translation of the Doctrine and Covenants and the Pearl of Great Price into the Korean language. He started his work in April and finished it five and a half months later, on September 25, 1966. The manuscript was typed by Sister Jung Shin Ja. This efficient and rapid translation was possible because Brother Chong had at hand materials translated earlier, including the Japanese edition, that he could read. He also had help from a reviewing committee set up by the mission president, composed of Chong Jong Chul, Ji Yong Dal, Rhee Ho Nam, Ch'on Nak So, and Han In Sang. This committee met regularly to review the translation as it progressed. Proofreading was completed on December 29, 1967. The manuscript went to press on April 8, 1968. Because President Palmer and family were released in early August, the project was completed under the direction of President Robert H. Slover, who presented copies to Elder Ezra Taft Benson and others at the mission home in Seoul, August 12, 1968.

The Language Training Mission

One of the most formidable problems faced by the

Presidency of the Asian-Pacific Language Training Mission: Kenneth J. Orton, center, first president; Loftin A. Harvey and C. Eugene Hill, counselors.

First group of missionaries to enter the Asian-Pacific Language Training Mission in Laie, Hawaii, on February 13, 1969.

Church in Asia is how best to learn to communicate effectively with the native inhabitants. Various sporadic efforts to train missionaries in Oriental languages of the Asian missions of the Church culminated, in late 1968, in the establishment of an Asian-Pacific Language Training Mission on the campus of the Church College of Hawaii at Laie. Kenneth J. Orton was called by the missionary committee and set apart as president by Elder Howard W. Hunter, with instructions to develop an organized program in Japanese, Korean, Mandarin, Cantonese, Samoan, Tongan, and Tahitian. Thai and Indonesian were later added to the list.

Operations began on January 10, 1969. New missionaries are sent to the school every two months for an eight-week study program. The first group of missionaries arrived in Hawaii on February 13, 1969, a total of eighty missionaries bound for Eastern fields of labor as follows: Japan-Okinawa, 10; Japan, 21; Korea, 9; Samoa, 11; Mandarin, 20; Cantonese, 9. A second group of 72 arrived on April 17, and a third group of 102 arrived on June 19. Six of these 102 comprised the first Thai language trainees. A fourth group of 86 arrived on August 28.

Thirty teachers are employed by the Language Training Mission and are under the direction of the mission presidency: Brother Orton, president; C. Eugene Hill, first counselor; and Loftin Harvey, second counselor. Each language group falls under the direction of zone counselors.

The eight-week schedule is divided into two levels. Level I (four weeks) introduces the missionaries to sounds, tones, pronunciation, grammar, syntax, pattern phrases, and specific dialogues designed for missionary use. The Level II (four weeks) phase emphasizes memorization of the six missionary discussions and a review of grammar. A Level III program has been developed to be used by missionaries after they complete the six discussions. Since the average number of discussions completed during this language training period is three, this program begins for most missionaries after they arrive in their mission field and continues until the termination of their call. However, advanced missionaries who complete the six discussions begin their Level III study prior to leaving Hawaii. Each successive group has been more successful than the previous one, and President Orton anticipates a maximum proficiency program to be in effect within one year from the beginning date.

The method of teaching is a combination of intensive audio-lingual and visual memorization techniques that take advantage of the years of research and experience of the Language Training Mission developed by Ernest J. Wilkins of Brigham Young University, the methods developed by Ermel J. Morton at Ricks College in Idaho, and their associates.

The goals of the Asian-Pacific program, like those at BYU, are threefold: first, to teach proper attitudes and a strong missionary attitude; second, to help the missionaries learn the fundamentals of the language they will speak in the field; third, to assist the missionaries in learning the six missionary discussions. At Laie there is also an attempt to introduce the various Oriental cultures to the prospective missionaries.

The initial approach and aspirations of the Asian-Pacific Language Training Mission were explained by President Orton to the mission presidents of Asia in a letter dated March 31, 1969. Excerpts from this communication suggest several basic problems and dilemmas connected with language learning in the missionary program of the Church:

> The inability to learn a foreign language is not the real problem, but the symptom of a problem. The real problem falls into one of two categories or possibly both. Category one — **attitude.** Category two — **aptitude.** If the problem is one of **attitude,** which usually results from various pressures, guilt, lack of self-confidence, sense of inferiority, insufficient humility, passive spirituality, inability to concentrate, or simply poor study habits, then we can attempt to identify the real problem and assist in formulating a solution. Once the problem has been identified and treated, the symptoms will disappear. In such a rapid and intensive program as that which we have here at the Language Training Mission, it is highly important that we identify the real problem early so that it does not detract from the elder's language learning process. Our emphasis upon special daily gospel lectures and inspirational talks is designed to create in the mind and heart of each missionary the image of himself as a true disciple of Christ. This is our first objective. Without a correct attitude everything else is pointless.
>
> On the other hand, if the problem is one of **aptitude,** then no matter how diligent, dedicated, or positive the missionary may

be, his effectiveness in a foreign mission could be greatly impaired and hampered, perhaps throughout his entire mission period. The problem of aptitude is not easily corrected. This does not mean, however, that it is impossible for a missionary with low language aptitude to be successful in a foreign mission. Conversion is a matter of the Spirit, and we all know of certain successful missionaries who were not highly qualified from a linguistic point of view. If steady progress and improvement is indicated, it may take a little longer, but eventually, disallowing discouragement, even the missionary with low language aptitude may become extremely effective. Having taken longer to master the language, he may develop a much greater appreciation for it.

Due in part to Kenneth Orton's perceptive and realistic leadership in laying the foundation of the language training program in Hawaii, much progress is now being realized in meeting the enormous challenge of communicating the gospel message in Asia, a highly important aspect of the Church encounter there.

The expanding influence of the translation services and the missionary language training programs of the Church in Asia and throughout the world are no doubt a wonderful fulfillment of prophecy. On March 8, 1833, a revelation to Joseph Smith the Prophet, given at Kirtland, Ohio, declared that "the arm of the Lord shall be revealed in power in convincing the nations, the heathen nations, the house of Joseph, of the gospel of their salvation." Then this far-reaching promise was given:

> For it shall come to pass in that day, that every man shall hear the fulness of the gospel in his own tongue, and in his own language, through those who are ordained unto this power, by the administration of the Comforter, shed forth upon them for the revelation of Jesus Christ. (D&C 90:11.)

XII

ASIA
Mission Presidents

Mission presidents in Asia with their supervisors from Salt Lake City: Front row: Edward Y. Okazaki, Japan-Okinawa; Elder Ezra Taft Benson of the Council of the Twelve; Paul S. Rose, Philippines; Robert H. Slover, Korea. Second row: G. Carlos Smith, Southeast Asia; President Bruce R. McConkie of the First Council of the Seventy; Walter R. Bills, Japan; and W. Brent Hardy, Hong Kong-Taiwan.

ASIA
Mission Presidents

JAPAN MISSION

Heber J. Grant (1901-03)
Horace S. Ensign (1903-05)
Alma O. Taylor (1905-10)
Elbert D. Thomas (1910-12)
H. Grant Ivins (1912-15)
Joseph H. Stimpson (1915-21)
Lloyd O. Ivie (1921-23)
Hilton A. Robertson (1923-24)
Edward L. Clissold (1948-49)
Vinal G. Mauss (1949-52)
Hilton A. Robertson (1952-55)

Northern Far East Mission

Paul C. Andrus (1955-62)
Dwayne N. Anderson (1962-65)
Adney Y. Komatsu (1965-68)

Japan Mission

Walter R. Bills (1968-)

Japan-Okinawa Mission

Edward Y. Okazaki (1968 -)

Japan East Mission

Russell N. Horiuchi (1970 -)

Japan West Mission

Kan Watanabe (1970 -)

CHINESE MISSION

Hilton A. Robertson (1949-52)

Southern Far East Mission

H. Grant Heaton (1955-59)
Robert S. Taylor (1959-62)
Jay A. Quealy, Jr. (1962-65)
Keith E. Garner (1965-68)

Hong Kong-Taiwan Mission

W. Brent Hardy (1968-)

KOREAN MISSION

Gail E. Carr (1962-65)
Spencer J. Palmer (1965-68)
Robert H. Slover (1968-)

PHILIPPINES MISSION

Paul S. Rose (1967-1970)
Dewitt C. Smith (1970-)

SOUTHEAST ASIA MISSION

G. Carlos Smith (1969-)

Index

Sangley Point, Philippines, 118
Sapporo, Japan, 5, 6
Sato, Chiyo, 68
Sato, Tatsui, 23, 65-69, 81, 84, 86, 182
Sato, Yasuo, 68
Savage, Levi, 127
Schull, William J., 84
Seoul East Chapel, 105
Seoul, Korea, 94, 102
Shanhaikuan, China, 32
Shimabukuro, Sam K., 72
Singapore, 51; dedicated for missionary
  work, 4, 157-60
Skelton, Robert, 148
Slover, Robert H., 82, 101, 112-13, 188,
  194-95
Smith, Elder, 101
Smith, G. Carlos, 160, 165-66, 194-95
Smith, Jessie Evans, 118
Smith, Joseph F., 71
Smith, Joseph Fielding, vi, 99, 101, 113, 118
Snow, Lorenzo, 56
Soh, William, 159
Soker Lee, 101
Southeast Asia Mission, 4, 51
Southern Far East Mission, 40-41, 49-51,
  121, 122, 135, 149
So Wan, 109
Srilaksanaa, Mrs., 134
Stimpson, Joseph H., 61-62, 195
Stout, Hosea, 27-29
Stum, Robert, 9, 14
Subic Bay, Philippines, 118

Taipei, 46-48
Taiwan, 4, 43, 46-48, 49
Taiyo Maru, 77
Takarazuka Motion Picture Studio, 10
Takeuchi, Hisado, 11
Tamanaha, Kuniko, 71
Tanaka, Kenje, 5
Taylor, Alma O., 57, 58-59, 179-81, 195
Taylor, John W., 56
Taylor, Milton B., 76
Taylor, Robert Sherman, 43, 120, 184, 195
Teeples, Karl, 47
Television show in Korea, 106
Thailand (Siam)
  American servicemen in, 4
  Bible in Thai language, 132
  characteristics of people in, 134-35
  Church in, 127-38
  dedicated for preaching of gospel, 129
  first baptism in, 132

first missionaries to (1853), 27, 127
hill tribe in, 136-37
in Southeast Asia Mission, 51
language and translation problems in,
  132, 135
missionaries return to (1968), 131
translation of scriptures in, 132, 135
Thirurhuvodoss, Paul, 149-53
Thomas, Elbert D., 58, 195
Tipton, Vernon J., 101
Till, Eugene P., 133
Tokyo, Japan, 60
Tokyo Stake, 3, 5
Tong, Sir Robert, 45
Tong, T. K., 84
Tracy, Lester, 121
Trail, James, 127
Translation, Chinese, 40, 47, 49, 177, 182-
  84; Japanese, 59, 177, 179-82; Korean,
  102, 177, 184-88; Thailand, 132, 135
Translation Services Department, 177
Tsubouchi, Jujiro, 180

University of Chicago Far Eastern Library,
  84

Vietnam, 4, 43, 49, 51, 107; dedicated for
  preaching of gospel, 141

Waddell, Lynn, 103, 184
Wade, Edward D., 30
Wagner, Edward W., 84, 85
Watanabe, Kan, 6, 10, 178, 195
Wayman, Oliver, 95-96
Webster, Canon Douglas, 20
West, Chauncey W., 127
Whitaker, W. O., 9-15
White, Larry R., 131, 136
White, Maurice, 147
Wilcox, Glen L., 131
Wilkins, Ernest J., 191
Willes, William, 147, 148
Williams, Gary, 87
Wingar, Robert W., 131

Xavier, Francis, 75
Yamanaka, Kenge, 78-79
Yokohama, Japan, 57, 60
Young, Brigham, 22, 27